VICTORY in ADVERSITY

R. Edward Miller, Author

Foreword

On the road of life it is impossible to walk without meeting adversities. Daily, many little niggling annoyances cross our paths. Conversely, there are catastrophic adversities that overwhelm the whole tenor of our life and send us along a by-road which we would never have willingly chosen. Such by-roads are usually thrust upon us much against our wills and desires. Nevertheless, "like it or not," the by-way stands before us. Our present road abruptly ends; the unpleasant by-road is set firmly before us.

Sadly enough, that by-road of great adversity is often considered "an evil thing" thrust upon us by some malevolent fate. Frequently, that troublesome road is made by the adverse acts of others; therefore, the consequences of their doings fall upon us much against our wills. Too many times we choose to blame people, devils or God for the adversities that come to us.

Whether or not we blame God, He takes upon Himself the responsibility and plainly says, "I did it." Although He may use men or devils, machines or sicknesses, accidents or casualties, God still basically accepts the full responsibility. Therefore, the reactions with which we face adversity focus on its Author — as well as on the more immediate causes.

The secret of triumph in any adversity is to accept God as its source, and to realize that God is infinite goodness and eternal love. All His works are done in lovingkindness and infinite wisdom. Because of this, I can rest in the assurance that God — who plans the affliction and brings it forth in my life — has done so with good and wise purposes. For God *is* good and wise; He ever seeks to bring forth in my life great good and blessing.

I cannot control the circumstances that bring adversity into my life, but I can choose the reactions with which I confront adversity. If I choose to react negatively — with anger, self-pity, bitterness and resentment — then I will negate all the blessing and advancement which God has purposed for me. Unfortunately, my negative reactions can defeat God's good intentions for me.

If, to the contrary, I kiss the hand that wounds, I thereby kiss the hand of God. If, with determined joy and love, I maintain faith and peace in my spirit and accept this trial as from His loving will, then I will turn defeat into victory and sorrow into triumph. I must realize that I am hidden in Him *in tribulations* as well as *in prosperity*.

To substantiate this principle, I have chosen Biblical characters who passed through deep valleys of adversity, yet turned them into triumphs of faith and hope. The lives of these believers shine on the pages of eternal history as lights which illumine the way for others. Their right attitudes and reactions in afflictions and trials brought forth into reality the blessed purposes of God, even in the midst of their sorrows and troubles. "'Tis not the gale but the set of the sail" that determines our destination.

These lives demonstrate that disastrous outward circumstances did not overwhelm them; to the contrary, their inward faith and hope, obedience and love turned their adversity into triumph. They wrested victory from the crushing jaws of sorrow and trouble because of God's power within them. Through His power, activated by their faith, hope and love, they refused to give way to doubt, despair and bitter hatred.

These men and women of God have greatly inspired me. I trust that as you travel life's road — meeting your own sorrows and trials — these victorious ones shall also inspire you. I have enlarged upon the details of their lives, taking cues from either the Scripture itself or else from human nature. As you read about their wonderful victories of faith in times of adversity, may their lives encourage you in your personal pilgrimage.

Contents

The Cilician Firebrand

A certain lad, born in a large port town on the Cydnus River in Cilicia, grew up in a Jewish community during a time when the Romans governed the city. His town was a holiday settlement built by the Romans near the beautiful Mediterranean Sea for their own pleasure.

If this Jewish lad were living in our modern age, we would call him a prodigy. In his early years not only was he physically energetic, but mentally, he was truly brilliant. When he began to show this precocious and phenomenal intellect at an early age, his parents and relatives concluded that he would become a true intellectual. And naturally, for a Jewish family, that meant he would most likely major in the field of Mosaic law and the Talmudic writings.

He Pursues His Goal

In his early school years, this lad, as was expected of him, set his mind and soul on studying the law, the prophets and the *Talmud*. For any Israelite, these writings and their accompanying rituals were their religion. As he grew older, he determined to become a lawyer and join that prestigious band of Jewish rulers known as the Sanhedrin which ruled in Israel in his day. Once he set his mind to this goal, he would never turn away from his chosen field. This de-

1

lighted his parents, for it was a great honor for a son to be one of the Sanhedrin.

After years of study, he graduated with honors from the local school. To attain his goal, he then had to go down to Jerusalem to study under the most notable masters. His good fortune was to become a student of Gamaliel, the most celebrated, brilliant and respected religious teacher of that day.

In Jerusalem he studied assiduously and his rapid development amazed his most prominent teacher, Gamaliel. Diligent and dedicated, the young student was indefatigable in his studies and rapidly became the pride and joy of his teachers. The more he studied and became knowledgeable in the law, the more vehement were the opinions he expressed. Being intense and fiery by nature in all that he thought and did, he formed immovable conclusions.

Outstanding Among His Peers

It did not take long for his teachers to realize two things: the lad was brilliant and intense, and he loved to argue. He was so fiery and opinionated that he lost few, if any, arguments. His inner drives to reach perfection — and to uphold his ancient religious traditions — were immense. Determining to know everything about God that could possibly be discovered, he studied even the most minute details of the history of God's dealings with His people. Every word and command that their God Jehovah had ever spoken by patriarch or prophet he meticulously mastered. He set an exalted goal for himself: he would become the last word — the final authority in the religious concerns of his people. He would equal his great master Gamaliel. Believing the sacred writings with all the intensity of his soul, he became extremely angry when some of his fellow students misquoted or misapplied any one of the Scriptures. And the more he studied,

2

the more jealous and zealous he became for the God revealed in their ancient and sacred writings. He fully endorsed the understandings of the Scriptures developed by his famous teacher Gamaliel, and received them as words from God. The youth was soon known as Gamaliel's protege; therefore few, if any, dared to stand against him in religious argument.

His fiery impetuosity kept him from becoming very popular with his peers, but that did not trouble him. In fact, the more he established himself in the higher knowledge of the law, the more he looked down on the less knowledgeable students and, for that matter, even the teachers. Being completely engrossed in his studies, he minimized the importance of social aspects of life. "They are really not all that necessary," he declared to himself. "However, at the same time, if the sacred writings impose some regulations concerning social demands, I'm quite willing to comply with them."

At long last, his goal was achieved; he graduated from his school with honors. His lengthy course of study was behind him. After his years of diligent study, the Sanhedrin accepted him into their celebrated body of eminent men. How elated and proud he was of his achievement! And being both elated and proud of his accomplishments, he now set for himself another goal — to become the finest scholar of that august body. Surely, it would not be too long before his name would become as well respected as the name of Gamaliel.

Tumult Over a Faith Healer

Satisfied when he reached his "life-time goal" of becoming a member of the Sanhedrin, he now became embroiled in the bothersome events that were daily distressing the people and causing them extreme unrest. The religious leaders were also deeply concerned because of the whisperings and arguments that were causing the people to take sides one against another. You see, this tumult was over a so-called "faith healer." A young man was performing unusual miracles which had been verified. In fact, even some members of the Sanhedrin had reportedly seen these stupendous miracles and admitted that they were true. Furthermore, the worst part was that a man — other than members of the prestigious Sanhedrin — had *dared* to bring forth new doctrines, ones not approved by this prestigious body. Up until that time, the Sanhedrin had held a monopoly, an absolute control over all religious matters. This miracle-working man had dared to challenge their supreme authority over the Scriptures. Worse than that, his miracles had excited and encouraged the people to believe in him. Some people were even courageous enough to say that this young man — Jesus of Nazareth — was God. What blasphemy! It was outlandish! How could a man — a mere man, even one who had performed miracles — be God?

War Is Declared

With well-calculated expediency, their religious leaders fought the fast-growing sect. Leaving no means untried, they marshaled their wrath against that blasphemer, Jesus, and worked to infect the people with their same bigoted hatred and religious zeal against Him. By guile and betrayal, they finally found Jesus in His prayer retreat in Gethsemane. They took Him prisoner and judged Him before an illegally called tribunal. They judged Him to be a vile blasphemer. His claims were too preposterous, too utterly intolerable for their "holy society" to accept. Therefore, by their holy law, the august Sanhedrin piously and illegally sentenced Him to death.

By imposing their will upon Pilate, they effectually did away with their most powerful rival by nailing Him to a

Roman cross. There, with deep satisfaction, they watched Him until He died. They worked diligently to insure that His tomb was effectively sealed. By doing away with Jesus, they were confident that they had terminated that horrid sect, and scattered His followers. "Let Him work a miracle now and come back from the grave!" they gloated as they mockingly laughed among themselves. In spite of all their carefully planned and executed measures, there still were some disquieting rumors circulating among the people. But they were only rumors — surely nothing more than mere rumors.

Even though the affair with Jesus had terminated prior to the young man's graduation from Gamaliel's school, he had been caught up in this furor of religious frenzy. His heart flamed with fury and hatred against the blaspheming Nazarene and His audacious and profane claims.

Rumors

Somehow, however, the "quiet" did not stay "quiet" very long. Rumors and more rumors buzzed around the city. More and more reports came to the Sanhedrin that Jesus of Nazareth had been seen alive in various parts of the country. Some of those reports must have come from ignorant dreamers; therefore, they could easily be discounted. But some whisperings came from sources that could not be so easily ignored. It appeared that Jesus was giving them more trouble after they had crucified Him than He had before. And the rumors grew and grew and grew. "Jesus has risen from the grave!" many said. Others reported that they had seen Him and talked with Him. Daily, "the Jesus sect" grew bolder as they gathered courage and strength.

What a preposterous thought! Jesus had been crucified. His death was a proven fact, although a few people still tried to claim that He had risen from the dead which was, of course, nothing but the dying gasps of self-defense of sadly deluded people. How could anyone believe such extravagant fairy tales?

Infuriating Miracles

Then to make matters worse, more reports of miracles came to the ears of the Sanhedrin. Some were even claiming that Jesus — the one whom they had crucified — was alive and had appeared to them. One rumor was especially galling because it happened in their very own *sacred temple*. That well-known beggar who had sat at the temple gate (for so many years) had been healed from his lifetime lameness. When the elders went to investigate the rumor, the man stood before them restored to health. They could not deny the miracle, for it was obvious and plainly visible to everyone. How it galled their souls to hear that ignorant beggar tell everyone that Peter and John (two disciples of Jesus) had healed him in the name of that "dead Jesus." Their atrocious claim — that Jesus had risen from the grave — could not be true; it must be a lie.

How it infuriated them to hear the lame man claim that Jesus had done this great miracle when they *knew* that Jesus was dead! How preposterous! In the history of the world had anyone ever escaped from the grave? Yet how . . . HOW in the name of common sense could these deluded ones use a dead man's name to do such a tremendous miracle? And the people — ignorant fools that they were — had utterly believed everything the disciples said. "These foolish simpletons believe the disciples' words more than they believe our solemn voices. How completely intolerable!" complained the Sanhedrin. "This must be terminated immediately. How frightening to see the hundreds that are joining that despised sect. It's utterly exasperating and out-rageous!''

War Renewed

These abominable and heinous doctrines must be — ab-solutely must be — stamped out; they are a direct attack on our beloved ancient religion and against our own inter-pretation of the Scriptures. ''These new and threatening doctrines must be excised immediately, once and for all. This whole heretical sect must be destroyed.''

As he listened to the many reports of this growing re-ligious heresy, the zealous firebrand — Saul by name — be-came increasingly angry. What a heinous insult to their God, to their religion, and to their religious leaders. Did not everyone understand that the members of the Sanhedrin were the only *real* masters of the ancient writings? What more was there to know? Who needed any addition to the Sanhedrin's wisdom?

Conferring with his old friend and teacher Gamaliel, Saul found to his consternation that the old man was amazingly tolerant. ''Leave it alone,'' he counselled, ''it may fall into the dust as so many other new ideas have. If it's of God . . . we want it! If it's not of God . . . it will crumble by itself. Why are you so agitated?''

Astounding Words Bite
Into Saul's Heart

Young Saul could not believe what he was hearing! What strange words coming from this most revered lawyer — from a man who was considered a ''teacher of teachers!'' ''It must be his age; he is too old to be on the front lines

7

anymore," Saul decided. Then to assuage any possibility there might be some truth in all that was happening, the youth quickly concluded, "Gamaliel probably won't be with us too long anyway." Saul reasoned that he could not afford to wait a bit longer, especially with this heretical sect running wild.

"Furthermore," he reasoned, "the Sanhedrin of today is responsible to preserve our heritage and our religion for our people and for future generations to come." The more Saul pondered, the more incensed he became. He accepted this new challenge to the Sanhedrin's religious expertise as his own personal battle. He MUST stamp out this heresy before it became a real threat to their ancient religion. "If this heresy continues," he avowed, "many of our more ignorant people will become completely deluded and drawn away . . . all because of a few sleight-of-hand performances and 'supposed miracles.' " As he poured over the details of what was happening, the fire of zeal and righteous indignation burned hot within his young breast.

Saul Seeks to Save His People

Saul made his decision. If no one else had enough courage to take aggressive action to destroy this heresy, then he, Saul of Tarsus, would see to it that something was done speedily. The Sanhedrin had laws to deal with cults. Saul's religion with its sacred writings, laws, precepts and commandments was life to him. The Scriptures were the air he breathed — the sum total of the words he spoke. He lived for his religion; he dreamed about it; he believed in it; he worshiped it. No one — absolutely no one — was going to introduce another religion which gave glory and honor to the name of Jesus, that crucified felon and deceiver. Imagine! Who would dare to propagate an erroneous religion

8

right under the very noses of the Sanhedrin?

Calling the officers of the Sanhedrin together, Saul demanded immediate action. "If no one else is willing to take action, then I will lead the way. Furthermore," he demanded, "give me a writ of authority. I will take some men with me to arrest and jail the men who are propagating this heresy. If necessary, I will examine them with the torturer's tools and slay those blasphemers wherever I find them." The fire of his zeal and the intensity of his jealous anger persuaded the Sanhedrin leaders. His collaborators promptly gave him the writ he requested. They also empowered him to use any method he felt necessary to stamp out this Jesus-sect, wherever he found it.

Those finely honed, serpent-toothed Pharisees found no difficulty at all in giving Saul the writ he requested because they, also, were highly incensed and secretly afraid of the way things were going.

These men, skillful in the law, lacked zeal; they recognized Saul as one who would act for them. Some of them knew many secret things that the young Saul did not know. There were many hidden factors they never told anyone about the death and strangely empty grave of that one called Jesus. Ah yes, there was that large sum of money given to the soldiers who guarded the tomb of Jesus. (Just a few knew about that secret and they were not about to noise it about.) Some very perturbed officers sent by the Sanhedrin to the tomb desperately wished that they could forget many things. Relentlessly, each man's conscience gave him no rest. Above all things, they desired this Jesus-sect to be completely eradicated forever. "Yes, Saul, you go out for us. Use any means you need to stamp out those followers of Jesus of Nazareth from the face of the earth."

Saul Seeks Victims

Feeling completely vindicated in his righteous indignation, Saul dashed out threatening dire consequences upon anyone ignorant enough to follow this Jesus-person. Saul swiftly vented his vitriolic tirade publicly. His threats soon reached the people — both believers and unbelievers alike. Because of his intense hatreds, it did not take him long to find victims. And as Saul apprehended believers and cast them into prison, pain and sorrow began to multiply for the followers of Jesus. Many prisoners heard agonizing screams in the stillness and darkness of the night, as Saul and his company pressured their victims to disclose the names of other Jesus-followers.

Saul and his band finally seized Stephen, one of the leaders of this sect, a young man about Saul's age. How surprised Saul was to find Stephen so educated, so thoroughly acquainted with matters of the Judaic law, so proficient and obviously well-prepared in his knowledge of the Scriptures. When this handsome young leader was brought before the ruling body and accused of heresy and blasphemy, Saul was present during the whole proceedings. How articulate Stephen was! Obviously, he was not among the intellectual elites; nevertheless, he was speaking as "an equal to equals." He neither quailed nor cowered in fear before that august body, but ably defended himself so skillfully that the Sanhedrin could not answer his arguments nor defend themselves against his attacks. Imagine! Actually attacking the prestigious Sanhedrin and accusing them of rebellion and perfidy against the very God they claimed to worship! Furthermore, Stephen accused them of treacherous betrayal and the murder of Jesus — the Just One. Confused, frustrated and convicted by their own consciences, they exploded in violent wrath; it was their only defense. They pronounced Stephen a blasphemer and immediately sentenced him to death by stoning.

The Challenge of
Well-Spoken Words

Marveling at Stephen's attitude, arguments and serenity, Saul became troubled because the rulers of the Sanhedrin had been totally incapable of effectively answering the young man's reasonings. The sting of Stephen's apology caused Saul to wonder just how it could, or if it should be answered. For legality's sake (as well as for the sake of Saul's peace of mind), an answer must be found. Stephen's words had challenged their law, their history and their religion, and his words must be answered! Being a keen reasoner himself, Saul recognized the dynamic force of the logic Stephen gave in his defense.

At that moment, Saul found it impossible to answer Stephen publicly — first, because he had no answer, and second, because the sentence called for immediate execution. Putting aside all his troubling arguments and questions, Saul's fury arose as he stormed against this heretical sect. With the writ of authority in his hand, Saul and his men bound Stephen and marched him out to the place of execution.

As the soldiers marched Stephen to a nearby field, the people began to pick up stones (not hard to find in the rocky land near Jerusalem). Many of the townsfolk who went out to witness his execution exclaimed, ''What a pity that such a handsome youth has to be so cruelly murdered. What evil has he done?'' Another answered, ''Nothing worthy of death.'' Stephen's only crime was that he loved and followed Jesus. Upon hearing what his crime was, the people grew silent, for many of them were also followers of Christ.

Angel Face

The aristocrat Saul did not lay his hand upon a stone; he let his men do that. His task was to hold the men's coats lest some thief run off with them. He just stood by and watched as the stones began to fly. Although the relentless bombardment found its mark on Stephen's vulnerable body, no stone touched his invulnerable spirit. Holding himself erect as long as he could, he looked steadfastly up into the heavens. And as he gazed upward, his face began to shine with an unearthly glow; he appeared to see *Someone* . . . suddenly he began to speak: "Lord, lay not this sin to their charge . . . Lord Jesus, receive my spirit" (Acts 7:59-60). Then he closed his eyes like a sleeping child and awakened beside his beloved Lord in the heavenlies.

"Did you see his face?" one commented, "it shone like an angel's face." Another added, "I actually saw light shining from his countenance." Someone else reported that as Stephen's body gave way to the cruel stones, his face began to change until it no longer looked like a man's face; it looked like the countenance of an angel from heaven. Silently and sullenly Saul remembered Stephen's words and his radiant face. In his heart was no rejoicing in Stephen's execution, for the people had all witnessed the young man's victory in death. His prayer of forgiveness for his murderers startled everyone! Saul's men did not rejoice that day, for they had seen and heard many things they were not expecting. The murderous men gathered up their coats and went home subdued and apprehensive.

Those who threw the stones were expecting Stephen to plead, threaten them with dire judgments, condemn them, and even blaspheme. In fact, Saul would have been delighted with this negative response from his victim. Had they not been justified in getting rid of this heretic? Instead, Stephen had prayed to the Lord to forgive them for their sin.

Stephen's words were incomprehensible to them; surely, their ears were deceiving them! And Stephen's face . . . that face . . . they could not get away from it; it haunted them. So terrible was the burden of what they had done that the next morning all of his hand-picked group of assassins came to Saul and resigned as part of his band. Saul found it necessary to recruit others to take their places. The impact of what they had done — and Stephen's unusual response to their injustice — raised too many unanswerable questions they were not willing to face.

Stephen's Remarkable Words

Saul's analytical mind was pierced and haunted by many unanswerable arguments and questions. "Oh, those dying words of Stephen! And that beautiful face — that ineffable shining face!" For the first time in his career, Saul could find no adequate answers, either in the law or in the prophets. He searched, but failed to find the answers he needed to solve this enigma. In truth, these mysteries troubled Saul far more than he cared to admit, even to himself. So to silence the tormenting questions, he impetuously rose up in even greater wrath when he heard there were more people of the same sect in Damascus. He immediately sought for another writ of authority to go to that city to stamp out this erroneous sect once and for all.

Gathering another group of fanatical young men, Saul set out for Damascus boasting vociferously that he would lay hands on every Jesus-follower he could find. When the announcement of what he was planning to do reached the ears of the believers, many were disquieted. "Saul, the Jesus-hater, is going out to search for more Jesus-followers. He is going to persecute them, throw them into prison and kill them! Then our lives, also, are in imminent danger," the people concluded.

A Blinding Light

The morning was bright; the skies were clear. Saul and his newly formed band set out early to avoid the heat of the day. Having left the walls of Jerusalem far behind them five days before, the band finally reached the oasis, stopping to take a much needed noon-day rest in this well-shaded wadi. They would reach Damascus in only two more days. What a relief! Their long journey was nearly over.

Suddenly, a blinding shaft of light shone from heaven and wholly encompassed Saul and his men. Saul was thrown to the ground as if a lightning bolt had struck him. But this was not a lightning bolt, for the blinding light engulfed them for a considerable time. As the light from heaven blazed upon them, suddenly, Saul heard a voice speak out of the thunder. While all of Saul's band could hear the thunder, they could not distinguish what the Voice was saying, nor could they see anyone. Only Saul distinguished what the thundering Voice was saying; "SAUL, SAUL, WHY PERSECUTEST THOU ME?" At the zenith of that blinding light was *One — brighter than the sun* — seated on the throne of His eternal Father in heaven.

Saul tremblingly answered, "Who art thou, Lord?" To his utter amazement the Voice answered, "I AM JESUS WHOM THOU PERSECUTEST!" No! No! A thousand times no! That glorious Being seated on the throne of Heaven could not be that same Jesus of Nazareth. It could not be! . . . Surely, it could not be this same Jesus whose followers he had been persecuting! It was too late for reasoning; the answer had already burned itself into Saul's spirit, heart and mind. "Yes . . . it is that same Jesus!"

The Strong Walls of
Tradition Fall

With that mind-shattering revelation, the solid stone structure of inherited religion came crashing down. The tradition that had taken Saul over twenty years to laboriously erect dissolved in a moment. Everything Saul thought he knew about God . . . His ways . . . His laws . . . and His prophets, was instantaneously cast down into the abyss of blinding ignorance.

Wrong, totally wrong was the mighty Saul of Tarsus! He had been living in error — awful, heretical, Christ-hating error. That brilliant student, the man with scholastic honors, the proud Pharisee, the honored member of the governing body — the Sanhedrin — was wrong, *wrong,* totally and utterly WRONG! The deceived were not Christ's followers; he, Saul, was the deceived one, stupid like a country dunce. Had he not been certain of his conclusions and beliefs? Had he not traced the line of the Redeemer so carefully through the law and through the prophets? Saul had proudly thought that he knew all the answers concerning the Messiah, but he had been wrong, so completely wrong! How could he have missed the truth so abysmally? How could the Messiah have been so hidden from his studious eyes in the ancient and sacred Scriptures? And how could so many brilliant minds of others in the Sanhedrin have been so stupidly blinded, when the very miracles of God testified to the Truth?

Error Exposed

Now what? Saul could never go back into that slime pit of deception. He had betrayed the trust of his God and his people. Not only had he been deceived; but he also was a deceiver. Persecuting the God he thought he was serving, he had tortured and slain the true people of Christ, the

15

Messiah. In unpardonable ignorance he had consented to Stephen's death. No wonder Stephen's life, death and apology had brought him to an unanswerable enigma! Stephen was *right;* he, Saul, his executioner, was *wrong!*

Under the devastating shock of his own false and iniquitous error, his keen mind reeled to and fro like a drunken man. Saul — the one who had prided himself in always being right — was now found to be devastatingly and unexcusably wrong! In blinding heavenly light, his soul exposed; his blatant hypocrisy now lay open for all to see. When light from heaven brought truth to Saul's mind, the blinders were taken off his spiritual eyes.

Saul Commanded to Go
to Damascus

Saul felt a desperate need to hide himself from the face of man. Finally opening his eyes, he found that his true spiritual state was now manifested in his physical being — he was blind. Of these things he was certain: Jesus was God . . . Jesus was real . . . Jesus was alive . . . Jesus was his Lord! From that moment on until the end of his life, Saul swore obedience to Him. He had no idea where he would go or what the Lord might desire of him. One thing was certain; he could never go back to the life of a Pharisee. His old religion was a School of the Blind where blind leaders stumbled around in the sacred Scriptures with no light to guide them. Now Saul knew that only with the *light of Christ* could he walk safely as "a lighted one."

Saul knew that he would fulfill the Lord's revealed plan, regardless of how long it took or how difficult it might be. His first obedience would be to go to Damascus to pray, and to wait on the Lord until He revealed the next step. Saul himself was born spiritually blind. When his eyes were finally opened to the divine light, then and only then, could he understand heavenly things.

God Reveals Himself

For the next three years the task of the analytical mind of Saul was to sort out God's truth. Little by little, revelation by revelation, and visitation after visitation of the Holy Spirit clarified Divine truths and brought them into order for him. As the rays of light released from heaven entered his soul, Saul wondered if he was in his right mind. He mused, "How simple. . . . How plain. . . . How could I have studied the Sacred Writ so thoroughly, and yet have missed truth so completely?"

As Saul diligently studied the Holy Writ, the wonders and mysteries of Christ shone clearly to him through the Scriptures. It seemed that every page spoke of Jesus, the Christ. "Oh, such blindness!" Saul thought. "How could I have been so utterly deluded? Jesus' sacrifice was plainly foretold; His works were explained. Why could I not have seen it long ago? Why did I have to cause such hurt to His church?" Time after time, remorse and repentance flooded through his soul. Could he ever forget how wrong he had been? Never again would he pridefully boast of his intellectual attainments.

Saul, the wretched deceiver, was dead — slain by a blast of light from the heavenlies. In Saul's place there arose a new man in Christ Jesus — PAUL OF TARSUS — AN APOSTLE OF JESUS THE CHRIST.

From Slave to Missionary

Narah is one of the most beautiful characters in the Bible.* She was a young lady, probably in her early teens, who lived long ago and would have been forgotten, had it not been for the excellence of her character and the strength of her simple faith in the midst of terrible adversity. They called her "Narah" in the original story and no one seems to know any more of her name than that. The Bible does not give any wealth of details concerning her person, family or home. All that is known of her must be deduced from the few astonishing particulars in this short narrative.

She lived with her parents in a small village on the eastern side of Israel where it shares a border with Syria. Evidently hers was a very godly family who carefully fulfilled all the observances called for by their religion, not in a perfunctory manner, but with a real faith, simplicity, and sincerity. Theirs was an uncomplicated life, for they had determined not to become involved with either the sophistication or the politics of Samaria, the king's city.

Hearing Ears

A man of God lived not far from their village, a prophet well-known and loved by many in the nearby towns. Whenever possible, Narah's family would visit the prophet and listen to his wonderful teachings about Jehovah God. How understandable, simple and clear these teachings were. Patiently the prophet explained divine things to them, and made God seem so very real, so close, as though they could always reach out and touch Him. This godly man lived and acted with the certainty that Jehovah (even though invisible) is a real person who ever desires to live close to His people. No matter where they are, God can talk to them — that is, whenever they are willing to get quiet enough to listen. "Just focus your heart and mind on Him," he would say, "and in the stillness within, you will be able to hear His voice."

Whoever came to the prophet, he would teach; wherever they invited him, he would go; and wherever he went, his message was the same: Jehovah is the true God . . . He is ever living, ever present. The idols you have adopted from your neighboring nations are neither true nor living; they are false and vain. As the prophet faithfully taught the people day after day, he diligently sought to lead them into paths of righteousness, and ever away from all that was unjust, unclean and sinful.

A Personal God

His teachings presented the principles and laws of Jehovah and the right ways to serve and worship Him. "Because God is a very personal God," he would often repeat, "He takes a special interest in each one of you as an individual; He wants to be *your* God, not only the God of priest and prophet. Because He is near you right now, you can call upon Him in every circumstance of your life, no matter what it is. He is a God of mercy who listens to the prayers of all His people. Furthermore, as a great God, the King of all the earth, the absolute Sovereign, He rules over the affairs of man.''

The name of this wonderful man of God — this teaching prophet — was Elisha. Since he worked so many wonderful miracles, many people were convinced that Elisha's Jehovah was the true God. Faithfully the prophet taught that God is not only longsuffering, merciful, kind and full of love, but He is also very just. Jehovah hates evil intensely and promises to pour forth judgments upon the wicked — when times of judgment are necessary.

Light in Dark Times
Brings Blessing

Because the period in which Elisha lived was a very wicked one, he faced much persecution and ridicule from the unbelieving people who refused to listen to him, and insisted on following their evil idolatry with its wicked practices. Fortunately, however, in spite of the stubborn ones, there were still some (not many) who listened attentively to Elisha's teachings. And as they listened, their faith was renewed and they were drawn toward righteousness. Not only were his teachings extraordinary, but the miracles that God worked in answer to his prayers were so astonishing that even the unbelievers could not deny that Elisha's God was a mighty God.

How different this God was from the gods of the fat priests in the temples. "Surely," the people concluded, "Elisha's God is a God of much power." And as Elisha faithfully taught them about Jehovah, their Father God, those who believed his teachings discovered Him for themselves. The God of their ancestors — Abraham, Moses, David and the judges — became a new reality to them. How wonderful to know they were also Jehovah's chosen people! Chosen! That wonderful God had chosen them — the God who had done glorious things. How proud they were! This realization made their faith stronger, and raised their expectations for His future workings. Was He not a marvelous God, a God who was their friend?

As Narah's family continued to meditate upon His ways, His laws and His judgments, they became increasingly aware of the wicked state of their land. Seeing all the evil that prevailed — and the many unbelievers in their own villages — they fearfully realized that if things continued as they were, God would send His judgments upon them. Terrible things would have to happen to awaken them and cause Israel to return to the true Jehovah God in spirit and in truth. Had not Elisha forewarned them time and time again of the judgments that their righteous God would pour out upon them if they refused to turn away from their wicked and evil ways?

Narah's family lived in a village with many affluent people who wanted absolutely nothing to do with Elisha or his message. They were too busy watching over their many possessions (and entertaining themselves with whatever amusement appealed to them at the moment) that they had no time to be concerned about God or His threats of judgment. Narah's family were not among the most wealthy, yet not at all poor. Because of their faith in the prophet's words they were despised and considered "odd." Their custom of always taking time to worship God and visit the prophet whenever he was near, brought the villagers' censure.

Dark Times Expose Weaknesses

At that time, there lived in the land of Syria a very ambitious general. Anxious to obtain a place — second only to the king in both power and importance — he determined to do many exploits so his expertise would not fail to be noticed. In order to gain this place, he would take a company of chosen men and send them out at night to attack and plunder some neighboring village, then carry away the rich spoils. As added booty, they would capture all the pretty maids to sell as slaves; the rest of the inhabitants they planned to slay. Their goal was to bring home the costliest and finest gifts, and then present them to the king. By this, the general thought to please his master and thereby obtain additional favor and prestige.

One day someone told this general about Narah's village — that it was wealthy, undefended and completely unwalled. "Why should we worry about defense measures?" the villagers concluded. "After all, war has not threatened us. Haven't we lived peacefully for so many years? Why should we worry about such things now?" Thus they continued spending most of their time enjoying life rather than cluttering their heads with the complicated and intricate strategies a defense program would demand. Having established no means to protect themselves or their goods, they argued that it was the king's responsibility to defend them. Surely, with all the taxes they paid, he should keep a battalion in their village exclusively for them. So with nary a care about the future, they spent their time arguing and complaining about how poorly the king managed his kingdom. "How selfish and autocratic he was! . . . Just think of it — not attending his people and their needs any better than that!"

After scouting carefully, the Syrian general decided to attack Narah's village on a certain night. His well-thought-out plan was to ambush the villagers, raid their homes, carry away their riches, and find a few lovely damsels for slaves. What a victory it would be if they could accomplish all this without any of the general's own men getting wounded! A surprise attack and all would be theirs. The general completed all necessary plans and preparations to attack.

Unprepared and Vulnerable

The appointed night and hour arrived. Suddenly — in the deep darkness and stillness of the night — wild threatening shouts of attacking marauders shattered Narah's village. "Syrian looters!" the people cried. Because they had made no preparations, Narah's terrified neighbors were utterly defenseless; therefore, they were cut down like grain before the scythe.

It was a night of indescribable terror and horror. Gruesome sights of slaughtered bodies were made more ghastly by the light of the ever-increasing fires that voraciously consumed house after house. Blood curdling death-screams shrilled through the village streets. Hellish laughter and loathsome curses of the raging warriors punctuated the scene of carnage. The end of their world came to the village that night as flaming fire consumed the dead and dying. In a few short hours the town ceased to exist; it was left but a heap of rubble. God's judgment had fallen. It was too late to repent; the time for repentance was passed. Only charred ashes marked the place where Narah's lovely village once stood.

Consequences of the Villagers' Blindness

Ere she had time to recover her senses, Narah found herself lifted up in the grasp of strong arms and flung across the back of a warrior's horse like a half-empty sack of grain. Hurting from the rough treatment and frightened beyond measure, she saw her own home catch fire as her captor rushed her away. There she lay, painfully pinioned in anguish and horror on the horse's back. As the marauder dashed away, he flailed cruelly with his sword, slaying anyone his weapon could reach. Even with Narah as an encumbrance, he still sought to do all he could to destroy. He and his companions had quickly destroyed all that had been lovely in her childhood: in moments it was gone forever. Her last memory of home was the sight of the bloody bodies of her loved family lying helpless in the cruel light of the devouring flames.

Gone was Narah's childhood, gone forever; gone were friends and fond possessions; and gone was her favorite baby brother who lay in the arms of death. Remembering the horror of seeing the mutilated bodies of her darling mother and father, she sobbed violently. All she had ever loved, all she had ever known, all she had ever wanted, all she had ever cherished was gone. Again the prophet's words proved true. But this time it was her own village upon which judgment fell. "I know we rightly deserved it," she sobbed to herself, "for we were so complacent and so wicked."

Words of Light Penetrate
Narah's Captivity

Like a healing balm, Elisha's oft repeated words came sweetly to her hurting mind and spirit: "Our God is an ever present help in times of trouble . . . He will never leave you nor forsake you . . . He will always be near . . . He will always hear your prayers." Throughout the night, as Narah lay across the horse's back, she prayed. And as she prayed, there came a healing balm of peace into her heart that she could not explain. Something deep inside whispered, "Fear not; all shall be well with thee, for I am here. I'll not leave you. Everything is under My control." Over her burdened spirit slipped a mantle of peace. Her heart rested during the remainder of the journey.

When they arrived in Damascus at dawn, Narah was thrust in with other captive maidens who anxiously awaited their fate at the hands of their captors. Strangely enough, Narah was not frantic and desperate like her companions; her words were not bitter, nor her lips filled with curses. Although she had been badly hurt and tears flowed easily, she found herself at peace. No burning hatreds or wrenching angers arose within her to trouble her spirit. After all, had her people not been warned? Had not the prophet foretold of divine judgments? Was not this her very own Jehovah God who had brought judgment upon them? Had she not discovered long ago that He was not only powerful, loving, kind and merciful, but He was also righteous and just — a God of judgment? And as she meditated, her heart sought and found consolation in her God. Surely, He would take care of her. Narah knew that all would turn out right. And Narah's faith in her God held strong in the midst of the burning fires of affliction and mourning.

Light's Warm Rays Bring Peace Amid Turmoil

Now it so happened that before they carried the slaves away to the shame and horror of the auction block, the Syrian general himself came to see what booty his marauders had captured. Looking over the pouting, angry, tearful and terrified group of captive girls, his eyes fell upon Narah. How different the expression on her face! Her peaceful demeanor and unnatural serenity surprised him. Walking over to her, he asked for her name. "I am called Narah, sir," she humbly answered. No hate blazed in her eyes, no sullen anger filled her voice, no fear distorted her pleasant features. She spoke serenely and honestly as though she were addressing an important family member.

The general took her by the hand and led her to the soldier who had captured her. "Is this one yours?" he questioned. "Yes, sir!" came the soldier's quick reply. Handing the soldier two pieces of gold the general commanded, "Here, take this! I will buy this slave now before the auction begins." Delighted — for the sum was far more than he could have gained for her at the auction — the soldier grasped the money and slipped quietly away.

As the general led Narah home, he found he was answering her questions in kindness rather than in the rough manner he usually used with his slaves. Nor could he explain to himself how he, the king's highest general, found himself kindly leading this unknown slave girl to his home. To bring slave girls home was the task of another slave, not for him, the king's most important general. He felt strangely constrained by something, he knew not what.

Peace — An Abiding Place

In this cruel way Narah was brought into the house of the highest general in Damascus. There she was given tasks along with all the other slaves. Surprisingly enough, from the very first, word began to spread in her master's big house that there was something special about this particular child slave. Everyone remarked about her inexplicable and extraordinary serenity, obedience, honesty and diligence. Unlike the others, she did not require the lash of the overseer, for she always fulfilled her duties without prodding. Into some of the stormiest scenes she was able to bring peace. Because her kindness and meekness also reached the other slaves, they did not resent her either. Narah had found refuge in Jehovah — the true and living God of her people. Under His loving watch care she discovered a continual abiding place. After the long day, when her tasks were finished, she could be found on her pallet of straw tearfully praying and communing with her Friend — the Jehovah God who loved her.

26

Peace Spreads Its Rays
of Warmth Abroad

What Elisha had shared with her concerning an intimate, personal relationship with God she recognized to be true. Her Jehovah God cared and shared all of her sorrows. He wiped away all her tears, and took away the sting and hurt from cutting words hurled at her from frustrated and impatient members of the household. She discovered the joy that did not depend on outward circumstances but proceeded from the heart of God Himself. Without any questions or doubts, she knew that God was on her side. And because she knew that His ways were right, she had no need to fret or be anxious when He sent His righteous judgments.

Little by little, the household became convinced that Narah — the little slave girl who believed so fervently in her God — was amazingly different; she was one who could be trusted. From her lips came no lies, and in the fulfilling of her duties there was no deceitfulness nor did stormy, sullen looks greet the harsh words of her superiors. With faith in her Jehovah to uphold her and with His peace in her heart to sustain her, she found no room for bitter vengeance and biting hatred in her conversations with others. In the secret citadel of her heart, peace and tranquility reigned. There she allowed no bitterness, self-pity, rebellion, hatred, anger or lust for vengeance to lodge. Little by little, the small Israelite captive had captured the confidence and trust of her captors.

Tragedy Strikes the Household

With the passing of the years, Narah (now no longer a teenager) had matured into a lovely and attractive young woman well liked by the whole household. One morning as she was serving the breakfast drinks and fruit to her master and mistress, she was amazed to see the anxious fear and sadness on their faces. Overhearing their conversation — for they had discovered that they could trust her — she heard the tragic news: her master had contracted leprosy! Oh, the tragedy of it — that horrible, disabling disease would destroy his life, his home, his career, his future.

Narah was overheard saying how much she regretted what had happened to her master, then added that she knew her God would heal him of his terrible disease if he could just reach the prophet. If he would go to Elisha and ask him to pray, God would surely heal him of this destroying plague. Narah's simple faith and trust in her God refused to doubt His power, even in the face of this dread and impossible-to-cure plague. She did not entertain gloating thoughts of a rightful vengeance against Naaman. To the contrary, she had a true desire in her mercying heart that her master might obtain help and find healing from the terror of leprosy.

A Surrendered Life Brings Rays
of Hope to Others

Swiftly her words reached her mistress and master who summoned her to come immediately. They promptly asked her what she had said concerning the possibility of her master being healed of leprosy. Had she said it? Was it true? Did she really believe it? "Leprosy is incurable, you know," Naaman challenged. "Do you truly think that your God is able to cure me? Does your prophet Elisha have enough faith and power to heal me from this dread disease?"

In Narah's prompt response there was no retraction. To the contrary, in simplicity and integrity she declared her faith in the mighty power of her God and in the ministry of His prophet, Elisha. "It is true that I said I believed Naaman can be healed of his leprosy," Narah replied. "I believe every word I said." Simply she shared with them how she had seen Elisha's words come true many times, and told some of great miracles he had done in the name of his Jehovah God. How sincerely she wished her master Naaman would go and find the prophet so that he, too, could be healed.

Such faith coming through lips known to be truthful — and from a merciful heart known to be without malice or vengeance — caused Naaman's desperate heart to grasp her words as a last hope. Narah's words must be true! Had they not witnessed her trustworthy nature over and over again? Had they not seen that she manifested no revenge against them, her captors, in spite of what they had done? Was not her life a testimony of triumph? Was she not willing to serve her God without complaint? Such a different life it was! They could not deny her witness, her winsomeness, nor her victory in adversity. Narah's life bore strong testimony to the verity of her words; surely, what she said must be true. Therefore, Naaman would travel to Israel to visit Narah's prophet to seek healing from his leprosy.

It was in this manner that Naaman the leper went to the king to get permission from him to journey to the enemy land of Israel. In amazement the king listened to the testimony of the slave Narah, and promptly granted permission to General Naaman to make a journey into Israel. This was not the journey of a warrior to do battle, but of a supplicant seeking peace and help from the God of the Israelites.

Obedience Brings Fruit

The story of how he found the prophet and was told to dip seven times in the muddy river Jordan is well known. How angry he became when the renowned prophet presented such a simple remedy! At first, Naaman angrily refused to heed the prophet's words. But fortunately, his servants patiently entreated and encouraged him to simply obey Elisha. In fact, they insisted that he obey. And when he finally obeyed the prophet's words, he discovered for himself that Narah's God was the true God . . . He was powerful . . . He was merciful. Thus Naaman became one of the few who were ever healed by the power of God from that dreadful plague of leprosy.

Truly, Naaman's story would be well worth telling, but this story is about Narah, the slave lass. Was Narah the slave of Naaman? Or was she the slave of her Jehovah God? Was she not one of God's first missionaries to Syria? Was she not sent into that foreign land and held there against her will to teach the Syrians about her true and living God? Did not her testimony and the witness of her own obedient life bring forth a miracle of healing in the general of the armies of Syria? Did she not teach that key household about Jehovah, the *I am* God, and turn them away from their idolatry?

Her life spoke much more clearly than her words could ever have spoken. Her commission from God was to be a witness for Him to turn the Syrians away from their dumb idols. Her's was a God-given light to illumine a pagan people, to reveal to them what she had learned of her God from the prophet Elisha. For it was there at his feet, as she listened in faith and in love, that she came to adore her wonderful Lord and trust in Him. Narah so treasured God's life-giving message that she hardly realized she possessed it.

Even in the midst of most terrible adversity, Narah, one chosen out of thousands, held fast her faith and trust in her God. The Lord knew beforehand that she would rest her case in His hands and trust Him to bring her out of the fiery furnace of affliction. He chose Narah to bring life and faith into the heart of a pagan idolater whom God healed. Because

Narah's life confirmed and upheld her testimony, this faith in Jehovah, the true and living God, was birthed in the land of Syria.

A Witness of God's Mercy

Triumphantly Naaman returned home completely healed; his leprous flesh had become as fresh and healthy as a baby's. What a glorious truth: Narah's God, the great Jehovah God, the God who loved His own chosen people in the Land of Israel, also loved the Syrians, even though they had been Israel's enemies and killed many of His people. Narah had been a faithful witness, a missionary who not only preached the love of God, but lived it — even in the bitterness of slavery. Her victorious life and testimony as a slave were the elements that gave "wings of truth" to her witness. When God tried her in the fires of adversity, she remained true to Him.

True Light Brings Freedom

When Naaman returned home, he called all his servants together to tell them of the wonderful things God had done. He related how Jehovah had marvelously healed him as he obeyed the command of Elisha to bathe seven times in the river Jordan. Clearly, and with many details, he shared how he had been converted to Narah's God — the one true God.

From now on Narah would no longer be their slave, she would be their honored teacher. They asked her to teach them the ways of her wonderful Jehovah God, and prepare them to love, worship and serve Him. Because Narah was faithful to witness to Naaman of her mighty God of mercy and power, they gave her the privilege of teaching the Syrians about Jehovah.

When the general told the king his marvelous story, the king was astonished; he could not deny this great miracle that stood in flesh before him. And seeing, the king also believed. This great God of Israel had been kind and merciful . . . merciful to a Syrian . . . merciful even to one of Israel's enemies! Of a truth, this God was not their enemy. Nor had Narah been their enemy. She had been a light in a very dark place. This great Jehovah God of Israel could also be the God of the Syrians. Seeing Naaman's miraculous healing, the king believed. And if the king believed . . . who would be the courtier so unwise as not to believe? Thus Narah was brought with honor even into the court of the king to tell him of her great Jehovah and of His righteousness and mercy.

Out of the seed corn that God planted in Narah's heart, there grew a faith that refused to abandon her trust in her God. In the earth of bitter adversity and slavery, the life of a true missionary began to grow. The horrifying circumstances in no way stifled the life of this plant, for God planted this living seed in Syria. Under His wise providence, this seed grew until it brought forth much fruit. A beautiful revival came out of a life of willing obedience and joyful submission. Narah, the slave, was Jehovah's first missionary to Syria.

Victory Over Circumstances

For the true believing children of God who love Him, ". . . all things work together for good to them that love God, to them who are the called according to His purpose" (Romans 8:28). It may sometimes appear that God has forgotten His own and that circumstances are under the control of the devil himself — or that God has lost control of the situation. It may appear that He is so loveless and inconsiderate that He isn't even bothering to extricate His children from their trials and distresses. However, *God is in charge of all circumstances* from the smallest details to the greatest. He does all things according to His high purposes, according to His infinite wisdom and fathomless love.

Narah's faith and works of obedience — in spite of sad conditions, puzzling situations, and difficult environments — demonstrate that even in adversity God can bring victory. The more trying, difficult and stressful the circumstances, the more glory God can bring as a result. The slave Narah depicts for us the victory of faith, obedience and trust in the midst of heathen darkness. The more intensely the bright lamp burns, the greater the illumination in the darkest of rooms.

In effect, Narah was saying, "I'm not offended in You, Lord. You alone are in complete control of all the events of my life. I have no complaint against You."

Did not the prophet Isaiah say, "For My thoughts are not your thoughts, neither are your ways My ways . . . "? So Narah rested her case in God and, as His slave, she walked before Him victoriously in a dark pagan land.

*In Hebrew, Narah means maid (servant).

From Dreams to Throne

There was a lad called Joe, the youngest in his family of ten. Although he was the darling of his father, he definitely was not the darling of his half-brothers. Perhaps because he was much younger than they were, he found it impossible to form a good relationship with them. Because he was his father's favorite — and since his tongue was not as controlled as it might have been — he often told his father of his brothers' mischief. Their jealousy of him, which increased daily, was augmented by their father's manifested love for the lad.

The older Joe grew, the more the half-brothers' hateful feelings increased until their resentments caused them to reject him completely. Their hatred and envy towards him intensified until there was no possibility of reconciliation. At the same time, his relationship with his father was growing stronger. Thus, though deeply loved by his father, he was utterly despised by his half-brothers.

Dreams and Truth

Dreams are strange things at best, and even today science is at a loss to explain them. Although some dreams are truly from God — which impart His Word and will to a man as he sleeps — most of our dreams are only the natural operations of the brain, or the results of either too much food or too strenuous activity. However, once in a while, as happened to the prophet Daniel, there is a dream or a vision by night that comes from God.

One night young Joe had a dream which he thoroughly believed came from God; there was no doubt in his mind. Truly, it was prophetic, and foretold future events. Shortly after his first dream, he had another which was uniquely similar to the first one. With simple and tenacious faith, he was certain that the two dreams — and his interpretation of them — came directly from God. In the dreams he saw himself as a ruler over his parents and his brothers who were bowing down before him in veneration and submission.

Reactions of Anger and Hatred

When he recounted the dreams to his family, his father was not too happy with them, and reprimanded him for entertaining such proud thoughts. And in addition, the dreams so infuriated his brethren, that their jealousy escalated to bitter envy and their anger to even greater hatred. How absurd! How preposterous! The thought that the favored one, the weakling of the family and the most despised of the brothers, should ever rule over them was too ridiculous and repugnant to even consider! It was worse than heresy. They would starve before they would ever bow one inch before him. Thereafter, in spite of all the brothers' ridicule and opposition, the lad continued to blithely believe his dreams had come from God. In the depths of his heart burned the faith and certainty that these dreams would surely prove to be true. Had not Jehovah God shown him in the dreams that he would rule over his family? Had the dreams not clearly showed his brothers bowing down before him? Therefore, Joe knew with confident assurance that it would be so, for God could not lie. He didn't know how, or when, or where the dreams would be fulfilled, but he was completely confident that they would surely come to pass.

Out of Control

At this point in time, the pathway of Joe's life went completely out of his control. Down into dark valleys of sad and painful experiences his path led him. Odd happenings, unusual circumstances and difficult situations began to form a chain of events which brought him increasing sorrow, pain and trouble. And it wasn't because Joe himself had done anything to cause these unwelcome things to happen. It all started so innocuously, so innocently. One day his father sent him to visit his brothers who had gone to the fields to care for their flocks in another part of the country. "Go," his father said to him, "find your brothers. See if all is well with them and their flocks, then return and bring back tidings."

Excited by the prospects of the adventurous errand for his father, the lad went out to the fields cheerfully whistling. Only after considerable searching did he find his brothers — who were far from happy to see him. When they saw him approaching, rage arose in their hearts. As they watched him walking through the fields towards them, they conspired together to destroy him. Away with this tattling dreamer forever! Away with his fanciful dreams of rulership over them! Finally deciding that it would not be wise to kill him outright, they plotted to throw him into a nearby pit from which he could not extricate himself. With this in mind, they waited. Concerning the pit . . . let time and natural causes do whatever they pleased to their brother. In this way his demise would no longer be their responsibility.

Cries for Mercy Fall on
Hardened Hearts

When the lad arrived in their camp, his brothers received him, not in brotherly kindness, but in bitter anger and hatred. Seizing him roughly, they yanked off his beautifully colored coat. Ruthlessly and roughly, they set into motion their murderous plan by mercilessly casting him into a nearby pit. However, when one of his half-brothers later saw a merchant caravan passing, he quickly conspired with the others to take their teenage brother from the pit, barter with the merchants and sell him as a slave. By doing this, they could get rid of him without bloodying their hands with murder, and at the same time make a neat profit.

The lad was broken-hearted and greatly frightened at such betrayal and treachery; his heart-rending cries for mercy availed nothing. There was no mercy whatsoever in any of his brothers' hearts; there was only hatred, resentment and envy. Even the deep anguish of his pleas, the shame of his betrayal, and the cruelty of selling him into slavery could not elicit from their hardened hearts one ounce of mercy. Joe's path now led him into an unknown future which would be filled with anguish; it was God's mercy that he could not foresee what yet lay before him. As the merchant caravan traveled steadily through the desert towards the southland, Joe journeyed deeper and deeper into the foul smelling slough of misery and hurts, loneliness and fear, prisons and lashes, chains and irons. His own brothers had sold Joe into slavery.

Given Over Into Slavery

Proceeding slowly into the deep south, the caravan arrived in Egypt where the merchants sold the lad to an army officer. There they branded him with his new master's brand and immediately set him to hard labor with scant rations. What a painful contrast between this place and his loved home so far away! This young slave differed from all the other slaves in that he believed his dreams had come from God. The God of Abraham, Isaac and Jacob who gave the dreams would surely fulfill them in His own time and in His own way. Instead of wallowing in self-pity and seething in bitter anger, he walked and worked with peace and tranquility acting as if he were a trusted freeman. His complete reliance upon the faithfulness of his God would not let either bitterness or resentment take up permanent residence in his soul.

A Different Attitude

In spite of the difficulties that came to him, Joseph's faith in the God of his grandfather Abraham held fast. He, the son of Jacob, would trust and accept whatever circumstances came to him from God without letting them defile his soul with bitter reactions and burning resentments. Everything that came to him he took as from the hand of his God, the Jehovah who always did all things well. His God — the Supreme Ruler over all things — was good; He could do no evil. Because of his faith, Joseph served his master with neither malice nor hatred. He served him with the same attitudes with which he had formerly served his own father — that is, with obedience, integrity, faithfulness and cheerfulness.

When his master noticed this unusual and welcomed attitude in his slave, he realized his good fortune in having Joseph. He began to increase his responsibilities, with the result that everything under his care prospered in his hands. Before long, his master promoted him to manager of his entire estate. He had full charge of all his master's possessions — the house, the farm, the slaves, and the cattle. In fact, he administered everything his master had.

An Enemy Plot

By now Joseph had grown into a most attractive young man. All went well until, much to his dismay, he became aware that his master's wife had become infatuated with him. As she tried in every way she knew to seduce him, Joseph did his utmost to avoid any contact with her, for he knew that this would bring him into great trouble. The woman's actions began to produce much tension in the household. Day after day he refused to yield to her enticements — she could neither seduce him nor bring him into her amorous net by her painted beauty. The more she pursued him, the more Joseph evaded her. When her frustration with him became unbearable, she determined to forcibly take matters into her own hands — to have him or else.

Finally the day came when her husband went away on business and she found herself alone in the house. When the handsome youth needed to come in to carry out certain responsibilities, the wife blatantly took advantage of the opportunity. The temptress — having tried all she knew and still failing to seduce him — boldly laid hold of his cloak and tried to force him to yield to her amorous intentions. It was futile, for Joseph was too upright to yield to her seductive wiles. When he broke loose from her evil and grasping hands, she held fast to his cloak. With a conscience free from condemnation, Joseph fled from the house. He left behind him an angry, scorned lioness implacable in her fury who now determined to destroy him.

Because Joseph had refused her, the spurned, angry and defeated woman resolved to wreak her vengeance upon him.

Waiting spitefully until her husband returned, she picked up the lad's coat. With her heart full of vicious lies, she approached him, showed him the coat, and accused Joseph of a terrible sin and breach of trust. She also lied to her husband about how valiantly she had resisted the young man's advances. This so aroused her husband's wrath that he refused to listen to Joseph's denial, but cast him into the chains and torments of the royal prison without a trial.

Joseph Becomes a Prisoner

In spite of anything Joseph could do, once more the hand of fate seemed to have turned totally against him. The more correctly he acted, the more evil seemed to be released into his life. His righteous actions, his faithfulness and integrity, instead of protecting him, only worked to cause him more trouble. On this occasion, his uprightness and integrity only resulted in his being cast into prison. How could his dreams ever be fulfilled when he lay helpless, betrayed, and abandoned in the dungeon of the king?

Joseph — A Different Prisoner

Fortunately, even in prison, Joseph refused to give up his faith in his dreams, or in the God who had spoken to him so many years ago. In the midst of these adverse circumstances, he steadfastly withstood the temptation to allow bitterness, resentment, anger, hatred, or any other self-destroying poison to enter his soul. His inward peace and positive attitude concerning the future came to the attention of his overseer. Joseph's attitude was unusual for a prisoner in chains and torments. When the warden noticed that no cursing came from Joseph's black dungeon, he concluded that this was a different prisoner, a better calibre of man. Having found the youth both true and trustworthy, the warden made him his trusted servant, placing him in charge of the jail with all its prisoners. In spite of his new responsibilities the warden refused to release him — Joseph remained a prisoner.

More Dreams

On a certain day, new prisoners were brought into the prison from the king's own household — one, the king's baker and the other, the king's butler. One night both of these men had strange dreams which so shook them that they recounted them to Joseph. To their amazement, the young man carefully considered the dreams then said, "I will tell both of you what your dreams mean."

"My God is pleased to show you beforehand the meaning of your dream," Joseph said to the butler. "In three days, you will be restored to service and released from this prison. And when this happens, please speak to the king for me, for I was unjustly thrown into this prison. I am innocent of all charges."

Then turning to the baker he said, "In three days you will be brought forth out of this prison, but you will not be restored to the king's favor. In your dream, you saw the birds eat the baked bread out of your basket; instead, you will be hanged, so shall the birds of the air consume your flesh as you hang there."

True to Joseph's interpretation of the two dreams, so it happened to both men. In three days the baker was taken from prison and hanged, and the butler was released and restored to service in the royal household. Contrary to his word, the butler soon forgot all about Joseph and his ability to interpret dreams. He failed to speak to the king, and because of his failure, Joseph continued to languish in prison.

Two more dreary, painful years dragged slowly by. Hurt and sorrow of continued confinement threatened to eat into the soul of the young prisoner. Nevertheless, he consistently resisted the temptation to allow either *hatred or bitterness* to trouble his spirit. "No matter what *those twins* from hell do to me they shall not penetrate the well-defended citadel of my soul!" he declared.

The Dreams of the King

One night, Pharaoh, king of Egypt had two dreams. Although he could not understand them, they so deeply impressed him that he could not sleep. He spent the rest of the night worrying about what they could mean. They haunted him, they pursued him, they harassed him. "I must discover what they mean!" he cried. "I must find someone with the ability to interpret them! Surely, the gods have spoken to me — of that I am certain — but what are they trying to tell me?" In desperation the king called the magicians and the soothsayers, but they proved to be as helpless and ignorant of the interpretations as the king himself.

With all the hustle and bustle of the comings and goings of the king's wise men, the problem of the interpretation of his dreams became common knowledge in the palace. Soon "everyone who was anyone" was asking himself, "Whatever can be the meaning of the king's strange dreams?" The commotion in the community stimulated the butler's memory. He recalled his time in prison some years before when a young fellow prisoner had interpreted two unusual dreams. Remembering that the youth's words had come true, the butler told the king what had happened. The king sent for Joseph.

Quickly releasing his chains, the warden brought him out

of the dungeon. Cutting and styling his hair, servants made him presentable, then rapidly brought him before the king who carefully scrutinized the handsome young man standing before him. Knowing that Joseph had just been released from prison, Pharaoh began to question: "Can this youth standing before me — just out of prison — possibly have the answers to my terribly haunting dreams? None of the wise men can help me . . . ? Can this foreigner, confined for years in the royal prison, have the power to solve the quandary of my puzzling dreams when none of my own wise men have any idea what these strange dreams mean?" Too perturbed to question any further, and ready to try anything to solve his dilemma, Pharaoh told Joseph his dreams. "Are you able to tell me the meaning of these troubling dreams?" he asked. "Can you give me a true interpretation?"

"O King," the lad answered, "of myself, I can neither understand nor interpret dreams. But the God of my father Abraham, whom I serve, shall give you peace by revealing the meaning of your dreams to me." Even as Joseph spoke to the king concerning his dreams, he was remembering the reality and truth of his own dreams of years ago. He still fully believed that God would bring them to pass in spite of the many negating things that had happened to him through the years. That same faith now gave Joseph the courage to answer the king. "Yes, oh revered king, my God has given me the answers to the mysteries of my own dreams of long ago; I know He will give me the answer to the riddles of your dreams."

As Joseph listened to the king relate the details of his dreams, he suddenly realized that God had been revealing what was going to happen in the coming years in the land of Egypt. The king's two dreams were but one. Certain of his correct interpretation, Joseph advised the king to make immediate preparations. "After seven very prosperous years in Egypt — with an abundance of crops — there shall come another seven years of terrible famine. The years of scarcity will be so bad that they will utterly consume the seven years of plenty.'' As Joseph interpreted the dreams, relief flooded into the king's heart — at last he understood the meaning of his strange dreams.

"What is so different about this young and handsome slave-lad brought from the prison?'' the king asked himself. And because Joseph showed such surety, serenity and faith in his own God-given interpretations, the king readily believed him. In fact, even as the king listened to Joseph's interpretation of his disturbing and distressing dreams, he knew in his heart that this interpretation was true. God was warning prophetically that extensive famine and miserable hardships were coming to Egypt.

Choose a Wise Man

Addressing the king, the prisoner said, "Choose out a man, who is discreet, honest and wise. Then let him make prudent preparations by storing up twenty percent of all the abundant harvest for the next seven years. Let him store the surplus of this bounty in large warehouses so the land will be ready for the coming years of famine when hunger will stalk the land.''

As Pharaoh carefully scrutinized his nobles, courtiers and chiefs, he realized that they were all too preoccupied with self-advancement, petty feuds and selfish political wranglings. Unfortunately, all were completely abandoned to the vice of self-promotion. Obviously, they had sold out their honor long ago. The king was convinced that in such a grand project as this — with its power and opportunity for fraud, cruelty and selfishness — none of his own men could be trusted. Who among his leaders would be sufficiently wise and unselfish for such an enormous and demanding task as this?

Looking straight before him into the eyes of that Hebrew slave, Pharaoh saw the right man — JOSEPH (the son of Jacob and the great-grandson of Abraham) who was unassuming, wise, serene, matured by sorrow and pain, yet not embittered. Obviously, he was a man who had a vision and faith for the future, for he had all the essential qualities needed to fill this place of power. The Lord had used the sharp instruments of suffering and pain to forge within Joseph's soul the necessary attributes for trustworthy leadership. With the cutting tools of injustice, hurt and sorrow, God had fully prepared him for this critical place of power.

The Role of Suffering

By royal decree Pharaoh raised Joseph to the highest position in the land, giving him authority, second to none beside himself. Joseph, the lad, the slave, the prisoner, at last reached his long awaited destiny. His strange and pain-filled path had faithfully led him to God's appointed place.

Using pathways of suffering and pain, God had built within the soul of Joseph all the necessary qualities required to occupy this place of power — so intricately laced with the snares of temptation and evil. God had fashioned a man with a heart of compassion, yet at the same time, with a heart as strong as steel in its integrity, wisdom, faithfulness, loyalty and honesty. With the sharp tool of adversity God had skillfully prepared a man to be His representative during the crisis years of a nation's history.

Ascended to the Throne

When placed in the position of highest power by the king, Joseph stepped into his destiny. The long, difficult, tear-stained pathway, unbeknown to him, had led him directly to the moment God had appointed for him. His faith had not been in vain.

For the word of God teaches us that if we are willing to suffer with Him, we shall also reign with Him. Whether it be a Joseph or a David, the true path to the throne is not by bloody carnage, inheritance, intrigue or politics, but it is through the pathway of pain and obedience. Faith that does not doubt — but is willing to accept God's dealing though the mountains quake and the hills be removed — is the Royal Highway. Not only did strange and painful happenings lead Joseph to Pharaoh's throne, but his positive, faith-filled reactions also prepared him for that place when God made it available.

By patiently walking the way of adversity — yet denying bitterness entrance to his soul — Joseph victoriously passed the hardest trial of all. Refusing to allow hatred, self-pity or lust for revenge to come into his heart, he was enabled to accept with grace the way God had appointed for him. He did not know "when" or "how" his faith would be rewarded, but Joseph believed his God would reward it.

No Vengeance in His Heart

When his estranged brothers — who had so treacherously set into motion all those painful happenings — came to buy food, Joseph did not fail the test. Instead of dwelling on their shameful betrayal, Joseph, now prime minister of Egypt, understood that their coming was a fulfillment of the dreams of his early youth. What happened during those days was an exact reproduction of the picture God had showed him so many years before. His brothers humbly came to him and bowed themselves before him. Though sold by them into slavery, Joseph was now willing to sell them the means to sustain their lives during this period of extreme drought. They came pleading for mercy and help — to the very one they had once hated and plotted to kill.

After their father's death, Joseph's brothers came to him fearfully seeking to placate his supposed hatred and to avoid his just vengeance. Joseph made a most beautiful statement of mercy and forgiveness; he answered their many fears by saying: "FEAR NOT, YE THOUGHT EVIL AGAINST ME, BUT GOD MEANT IT UNTO GOOD. . . ."

By carefully preparing His servant years ahead of time, God was wisely providing a place of sustenance for Abraham's seed during famine years. During their time in Egypt, God meant for them to grow, prosper and become a great nation. God found a man of tenacious faith, and then prepared him in the furnace of great affliction and adversity. He became a man that power could not corrupt — a man whom God could trust to be a true saviour to His people — even to those who had so mistreated him.

The Difficult Path
to the Throne

There are many pathways in life. Each one leads to a different destination: paths to success, to defeat, to monetary gain, to poverty, to fame, to power, to knowledge and to ignominy. There are times when a man is able to choose the path he will walk in life; at other times, however, his life path is marked out for him beyond his control; nevertheless, each man will walk his own pathway of life unto its destination.

In any pathway there always will be numerous happenings and numerous choices. The end of God's chosen path for a life is not an inevitable destination. No single happening can take a person away from the chosen destination of his path of life. Although some happenings will be pleasant, some unpleasant, and others most disagreeable, each new event presents a *choice of reactions*.

Reactions Are a Crucial Factor

The truly decisive factor is called "REACTION." A person's reactions to the incidents, environments and happenings of life are powerful forces that can drastically change a man's destination. For a believer, there are no good or bad happenings in themselves; but there are good or bad reactions to what happens. The Bible says: " . . . all things work together for good to them that love God, to them who are the called according to His purpose" (Romans 8:28). Jesus said that it is not what enters into a man that defiles him, but that which comes out of a man. Events come TO a person; reactions come OUT FROM him in response to the things that occur.

God has many mysterious ways that lead straight to the throne. Not always does the pathway lead through war and carnage. Nor is the pathway to the throne necessarily given to those who are born in a palace. Joseph's pathway to the throne led through painful and evil happenings. His right reaction to these determined his glorious destination.

Another Joseph

Centuries later, another Joseph came who also held tightly to God's promises that He, too, should reign in an everlasting kingdom. His Father sent Him on an errand of mercy to visit His half-brothers in a far-off place. That visit began a chain of painful and sorrowful events which took the pathway of His life out of His own control.

Without cause men hated and rejected Him. Despised by His brethren, He suffered because of their jealousy and envy. Betrayed by His own, He was taken captive and unjustly cast into prison. Then, without fair trial, He was condemned to death (though He had been declared innocent before both ruler and brethren). He was mercilessly slain and hung upon a cross by His own half-brothers.

Jesus, our Heavenly Joseph, even as young Joseph of old, refused to open the gates of His soul to bitterness, hatred, wrath or vengeance. And when He was crucified on that awful gibbet, He spoke words of highest mercy: "FATHER, FORGIVE THEM, FOR THEY KNOW NOT WHAT THEY DO." Truly, His were the responses and reactions of a King, and not of a felon. When He died that day, His faith in the word of His Father stood firm; He refused to doubt. He believed fully that His path would lead to the throne even as His Father had promised!

Heavenly Joseph Enthroned

Dead? Yes, for three days He lay in the grave. Then in the mighty power and glory of His kingship, Jesus arose — even as Joseph who stepped forth out of prison purified and prepared in fresh raiment. Through the bitterness of pain, through the agony of death, through the blackness and darkness of the grave — His faith in His Father did not fail. In glorious victory His faith triumphed as He arose again from the grave to take unto Himself the might and glory of His kingship.

This Eternal One stood in the midst of His brethren with

49

a glorious spirit of mercy, not a spirit of vengeance. When we, as His fearful and sinful brethren, come before Him — deserving nothing but His vengeance — our Saviour holds out the scepter of pardon. What amazing grace! Even though we had such a shameful part in making His feet trod that awful pathway to His kingdom, He still receives us in love. In our Divine Joseph, we find a heart full of mercy — a heart that warmly accepts us into His household where He promises to care for us forever. And even as Joseph's half-brothers found mercy when they came trembling into Pharaoh's court, expecting retribution for their sins, so shall we find mercy and pardon and sustenance in the person of Jesus *our Heavenly Joseph.*

Our God had preordained that His Son — as the Joseph of long ago — should go ahead to prepare the way of life for His chosen people. Had not our Heavenly Joseph walked this pathway of great pain to His throne, all His family would have perished in the judgments decreed over the land of their sojournings. Rejoice, believing pilgrims! Our Joseph sits on His eternal throne as our surety . . . our strength . . . our defender . . . our provider . . . and our merciful Saviour.

The Widow Evangelist

Almanah, as they unsympathetically called her, was well known in her small town where "everybody knew everyone else."* In spite of the fact that she was an energetic, hard-working woman, the lines of suffering on her face — caused by life's hard buffetings — made her look much older than she really was.

There was a time when she was a comely, vivacious young woman who lived happily with her kind husband and baby boy. Life was good to the little family who hoped and dreamed of a better future. By working hard and being frugal, they had saved enough to buy their small farm and comfortable little house. Yes, someday — if they were careful and industrious — they would be comfortably secure.

Changes Came Unexpectedly

Daily, Almanah went to the village well to draw water, to listen to the chatter of the other women, and to watch the camaraderie. Occasionally she joined the other housewives to wash clothes at the nearby village stream. Although the little stream continued to flow on and on, nothing could wash away from her heart the terrible memories of one tragic day. Playing and laughing with her baby, carefree and content, she suddenly heard great clamor outside. A large group of neighbors shouted as they came through the field to her house. Running pell-mell to her door, they called her with voices full of fear and anguish. Some terrible thing must have happened, but Almanah couldn't imagine what. ''An accident!'' they all exclaimed at once.

Before she could collect her senses, they rushed into her house carrying the dead and mangled body of her husband. ''An accident,'' they repeated as everyone tried to talk at once. The details of exactly what had happened were not entirely clear. While her husband was plowing with his oxen, he unearthed a wasp's nest. The usually docile oxen suddenly became completely unmanageable. In the mad, mindless scramble to escape the stinging pain, her husband had become tangled in the guide rope and had fallen. Trampled by the oxen and mangled by their wild cavortings, he was dragged many rods before the animals could be stopped. When the men finally reached her husband and were able to release him, his body was so torn that life had already been driven from it.

In one brief hour, Almanah's whole life had been destroyed and her lamp had gone out. Her darling husband, loved since childhood, was torn from her side in an instant without even a final farewell. Gone were all her dreams of the future; gone were her former hopes for a better life. In fact, that day she wished there would be no future for her. And had it not been for her baby, she probably would have ended her own life, as well. To her the shock and pain of this sudden tragedy were almost unbearable.

From that day on her neighbors called her Almanah the widow. Her place in the village social structure changed then more drastically. Set apart by fearful tragedy, she was truly no longer ''one of them.'' After her husband's death, the women of the town shunned her for fear that somehow her tragedy might contaminate their lives, also. Her neighbors believed her guilty of having incurred their gods' displeasure. True, she had been feared and avoided even before that terrible day, but when widowhood came suddenly upon her, fear and suspicion turned into distrust and open dislike.

In their ignorance, the women blamed her for that tragic event. After all, had not the priests of Baal and Molech warned that great trouble would come upon her? Without doubt she had made these gods angry with her strange ways. Why else would such an unusual and terrible thing happen to her? Their priests had foretold dire happenings; quite often they had warned her because of her beliefs. Now the villagers could truly say, "See, we already warned you that you were making our gods angry!" From then on, she was an outcast, a pariah, a woman of much sorrow — a widow set apart from her neighbors forever because of her grief and irreparable loss.

Almanah Discovers Jehovah

Some years before, when Almanah was a young girl, her parents made a business trip to Jerusalem, taking her with them. There she became enamored with the beautiful temple dedicated to the worship of Jehovah — the God of the Israelites. Intrigued by what she was discovering, she asked many questions about the God, Jehovah. Never before had she heard such wonderful things about any other god.

The more the people talked about Jehovah, the more Almanah realized how very different He was from her own cruel gods who were always angry and doing awful things to her people. Worst of all, back home the priests who served these cruel gods were wicked. They were known as the most loathsome people of the village. Because they could call the wrath of their gods upon anyone who offended them, everybody feared them.

As she learned more about Jehovah, she discovered that

He was completely unlike all the other gods. How the people of Israel loved and respected their priests! And how they loved their God and believed that He truly loved them! Entranced by the fascinating history of Jehovah's works among His people, Almanah never tired of listening to the stories of the marvelous miracles He had done. Their God, who cared for them as a faithful and devoted Father, had saved them with His mighty hand from Egyptian slavery. After leading His people through the Red Sea, and delivering them time after time in miraculous ways in the desert, He made of them a mighty nation. Throughout their history their God had prepared outstanding heroes of faith. He also had sent anointed prophets who did wondrous works in His name, and spoke His words to the people. "Yes," Almanah thought, "how easy it would be to learn to love a God like that."

The more she heard about Jehovah, the more her receptive child's heart believed. By the time her parents took her home to Zarephath, a new God was swelling within her heart. Never again would she believe in her old gods, Baal and Molech, nor would she join in pagan worship, for the practices of the priests made her feel miserable. Now, she would pray to her new God, Jehovah, just as she had learned to do in Jerusalem.

Almanah at Home

Instead of worshiping at the heathen temples with her neighbors, she could now pray to her new God, Jehovah. Her husband, who loved her dearly, affectionately tolerated her different religion and ways of worship. As Almanah shared with him what she remembered about Jehovah, he agreed with her that this God was surely much better and greater than their own gods. Nor had he paid any attention to the whisperings of the villagers who claimed that dire consequences would come upon her because of the anger of the gods. "Surely, terrible things will happen," they had said, "because Almanah has turned her back and spurned all the gods who have been our gods for centuries."

Long after that tragic day, the village women still openly accused her of having killed her husband by not worshiping their gods. In spite of their tormenting insults and accusations, Almanah's faith stood true, for she had learned to love and trust her kind God, Jehovah. The people still continued to reject and blame her, and she found it impossible to convince any of them of her innocence.

Famine — A Test of Faith

Almanah the widow now struggled on alone, working her small farm with whatever help she could find. Fearing even to be with her because she did not believe in their gods, her neighbors all refused to help her. Was she not living in danger from the wrath of these gods? And wouldn't anyone who befriended her also incur the anger of these gods? So Almanah walked on alone, daily struggling to keep her little home together for her son and herself. This child was all she had left; he was her husband's seed — the one she must carefully nourish lest the family name die out.

It became increasingly more difficult to make ends meet and to provide necessary bread. Then one year the spring rains failed. And when no rain fell to bring life to the seeds she had planted, not one of them sprouted. Fear began to enter everyone's heart. At first, the villagers blamed Almanah for what was happening. However, when they heard that all the surrounding towns and countries had also missed the spring rains, they thought the gods must be angry with all the people, not just with Almanah.

Not only did the spring rains fail, but the autumn rains, also. Because of the fear that now ruled in the hearts of the people, everyone offered many religious sacrifices to their gods. In spite of the many useless prayers which were offered begging the false gods to send the rains once again, the rains still stubbornly refused to fall. When during the next year the rains again failed, the people's fears turned into panic. Now, the source of bread they so desperately needed to sustain life was gone.

Many died of hunger — the old, the sick and the weak. The poor, who had no money to cushion their tragedy, were especially vulnerable. The situation was simple: if there was no money, there was no bread. And no one was giving anything away in these perilous times.

Pressures Come

Almanah began to feel the pressure. No matter how frugal she tried to be, her own storage bins slowly ran out. Little by little her possessions melted away. First, she sold some of her slaves. Were they not extra mouths to feed? She could not even sell the last slaves, for no one wanted to feed anyone else. During these months of drought, many slaves and hired servants were dismissed and given freedom to fend for themselves — either to live (if they could find the means to sustain life), or to starve.

Next, Almanah had to sell all her livestock. When the last oxen were sold, she despaired, knowing she could no longer till her land even if the rains should come. As the terrible famine continued, she found it necessary to sell most of her land, an action which temporarily staved off hunger. Because a few rich folk owned almost all the land of the village, the poor became increasingly impoverished. After that, Almanah's furniture had to go, even cherished heirlooms which had been handed down from her great-grandparents. Life itself had become more precious than anything she possessed.

Little by little, the famine consumed everything she owned; soon there was nothing left. Even though the family had lived as frugally as possible, and Almanah had scavenged diligently, not even a weed remained that was edible. When the second year of scarcity came (and no one could anticipate how long the drought would last) everyone contemplated the future with dread.

In spite of anything anyone could do, the death toll mounted. Every morning villagers wearily carried dead bodies out of the city for carrion birds and jackals to consume. The mourners loathed the situation, but there wasn't much they could do, for the weakened villagers had no strength to bury their dead.

Almanah Faces a Final Test

Finally, as Almanah sadly looked around her dwelling, she realized with trepidation that the dread day had finally come — she had nothing left to sell. Jewels, furniture, land, livestock . . . everything sellable was gone; her cupboard was bare. Only sufficient flour for one more frugal meal remained — and scarcely enough oil to bind the ingredients together for baking. That was it! She and her son would eat their last meal together, and then . . . and then, quietly wait for death; there was nothing left to do. Hope had fled. The little widow could do no more. She had done what she could, but what could prevail against this terrible famine? Almanah resigned herself to the mercies of her Jehovah. If her miracle-working God would save her . . . if not, she would go to meet Him in Paradise. Surrendering herself unto His hands, she prepared to go out to find a few sticks so she could bake her last cake.

Months of drought had relentlessly propelled Almanah to a bitter end. She now had but one more cake — this was the *cake of truth,* the cake of reality, the stark and harsh reality that she had reached the end of all her own resources. She had done all that was possible; there was nothing left for her to do. In no way could she save herself; only Jehovah God could save her now. The family's future was in His hands. If He would save them, they would live. If not, they would die. There was absolutely no way for Almanah to save herself. Surely, the hour had come when she and her son would eat their last meal and then die together. All hope had fled; there was nothing to look forward to but despair, starvation and death.

With that understanding came the realization that Jehovah, the God of the Israelites, was the only One to whom she could turn — the only One in whom she might hope. In spite of all the terrible things that had happened, she was *not offended* in her Lord. Neither could she understand what was happening, for rumor claimed that all Israel (not just her village) was also under the lash of that terrible famine. It was, she was sure, too great a famine for the gods of the land to do anything about, but she was certain that her Jehovah could change the situation if He wished to. Or could it be that He, too, was angry because of the evil and unrighteousness that reigned in the land?

It was mid-morning when the little widow began to search for a couple of sticks to kindle a small fire to bake their last cake of bread, and then prepare for the death that would mercifully deliver them from further suffering.

Too wasted to fret or be anxious, too sad to complain, and too weak to really care, she slowly left her house to look for fuel to cook today's meager meal. As she searched here and there, she saw a stranger who called to her, "I say, would you please bring me a cup of water that I may drink?"

A Willing Heart Meets
Jehovah's Prophet

Willingly she started towards home to fetch a cup of well water (very hard to get now, for the well only seeped out water little by little; in fact, most of the time only the early riser found any water at all). Before she had gone very far, the stranger again called to her, "I say, lady, would you also bring me some bread to eat?" Surely this was a serious and strange request in this time of famine! There were no handouts to give to anybody, least of all to strangers. Because no one had anything to share, the needy were left to die alone. While Almanah was ready to share a cup of water, was she ready to give up her last small piece of bread?

Answering, neither in bitterness nor in irony — but in the refreshing simplicity of truth — she exclaimed, "I don't have a loaf of bread; I only have a handful of meal in my meal-barrel and a little oil in a cruse. Even now I am gathering two sticks that I may go and cook the last meal for my son and me that we may eat it and then . . . die!"

With an urgent tone in his voice, the stranger said, "Don't be afraid. Go and prepare the food like you planned to, but bring me a cake first. Then, after I have eaten, you may prepare bread for yourself and for your son. Jehovah — the God of Israel — is speaking to you and He is saying, 'THY BARREL SHALL NOT WASTE, NEITHER SHALL THE CRUSE OF OIL FAIL, UNTIL THE DAY THAT JEHOVAH SENDETH RAIN UPON THE EARTH.' " Addressing her once again, he added, "FEAR NOT, FOR JEHOVAH, THE GOD OF ISRAEL SAYS THAT YOU SHALL LIVE AND NOT DIE."

Jehovah's Words Bring Renewal
to a Weary Heart

The stranger's words entered her spirit like rays of light. Faith sprang up like a fire kindled by a bolt of lightning. ''My God has spoken concerning me! He has heard my many prayers . . . He has not forgotten me. Jehovah sent His prophet specifically to me — even though I have not even heard His name spoken in faith since my childhood.''

Faith lent wings to her feet and she swiftly brought him water. Then, after inviting the prophet into her home, and asking him to stay for as long as he desired, she ran out and soon found the needed sticks. With a strange peace and joy in her heart, she quickly mixed the oil and meal and baked him a cake. No sooner had the stranger eaten than she went to her meal-barrel. Amazed, she found there was sufficient meal in the barrel and oil in the cruse to make another good-sized cake. For both Almanah and her son there was sufficient to eat.

The rest of the day she spent communing with the prophet whose name was Elijah. How many questions he answered for her! Yes, it was Jehovah, Himself, who had sent the famine because He wanted to bring His people back to Himself. In fact, He was working to deliver them from their foreign gods, and from all their evil ways. Quickly the hours sped by as the prophet told her more about the beloved Jehovah to whom she had been praying all those years.

The next morning there was enough meal in the barrel for the three of them. And in the cruse, again there was enough oil. Jehovah had worked a miracle of life for her right there in her home. And even better yet, He had sent a prophet to her who would teach her and her son all about the worship and ways and laws of Jehovah.

Jehovah's Provisions Sustain
the Hungry

Joy — a joy like she had never known before — came flooding into her soul. Day after day, and month after month, Jehovah renewed her barrel of meal and replenished her cruse of oil. And now, even in the midst of the terrible crisis, Almanah continued to experience overflowing joy. Throughout the drought she always had sufficient food and drink, even though many tragedies surrounded her (for during the time of famine, death was having "a field day").

In her village, and in the surrounding towns, death reigned. High and low, rich and poor, strong and weak — all were stolen away by the enemy's destroying hands. However, in Almanah's home, life reigned; health and strength were her daily portion. The prophet taught her about the wonderful mercy, grace and goodness of Jehovah. As God vindicated her in the eyes of her detractors, her enemies disappeared. Now, Almanah's neighbors who continually watched her could not help but marvel at her daily miracles.

Because Almanah was in excellent health, she never became weary, nor did she weaken. How could she ever explain to others her decision to provide a home for this strange visitor during famine times? She had no stores of food that anyone could see. When her neighbors would visit, and peek curiously into every nook and cranny, they would find nothing. The people wondered, for Almanah and her little household were so full of abundant strength and energy. "Most evidently," they concluded, "there must be a miracle taking place every day at Almanah's house."

Elijah, the Evangelist

Nor did Almanah seal her lips; she proclaimed far and wide the beautiful things her God was doing for her. Anyone willing to come to her house was invited to hear the prophet who tirelessly taught about the wonderful God, Jehovah. Because they beheld the miracle of life and health in Almanah and her son, they listened attentively and received Elijah's words. Those who heeded the prophet's words were convinced. Believing, they turned away from their heathen gods, and trusted in the true God — Almanah's God — the Jehovah God of Israel.

The Life-Giving Rains Return

Finally, the day came when God again spoke to Elijah and told him that it was time for the rains to return. "Make ready," he commanded, "your fields will bloom again; the earth will bring forth its fruits because the rains are coming! The famine will be over!" After bidding Almanah farewell, the prophet departed to go to Carmel. There, in obedience to Jehovah, he called down the rains upon the thirsty land — rains that proceeded from the merciful hand of the mighty Jehovah God.

When Elijah went to Carmel, he left a small company with Almanah, the widow who believed. By working together, Almanah and her friends helped each other. Even before Jehovah sent the rains as He had promised, they managed to find some seed and plant their remaining fields. And because they planted before the rains came, theirs were the first fields to harvest. God vindicated their obedience, and confirmed their faith.

As for Almanah's town, it was no longer a place where Baal or Molech were worshiped. The people had come to know and to believe in the one and only true God — Jehovah, the God of Israel. Almanah was no longer despised nor blamed for the troubles of the village. To the contrary, she became their highly respected teacher in the ways of Jehovah. Had she not spent over a year sitting and learning at the prophet's feet? Now, she was able to teach others the beautiful truths she had learned.

Even when stricken by adversity, Almanah maintained her faith in Jehovah, and became an encouraging example of those who trust in Him and wait for the fulfillment of His promises. When believers pass through deep waters, trials do not destroy them, for God has promised to care for them. In this way, the little widow became a source of inspiration to her people — a living testimony of how the Lord will save His church and sustain it even in times when the rains fail.

God Provided Meal and Oil

When Elijah came to stay with her, Almanah still had the essentials for life in her home till the very end of her trial. By the end of the famine almost everything was gone, sold or forgotten — but Almanah still kept the oil and the meal. Meal speaks of Christ, the Word, and oil speaks of the Holy Spirit. Even when everything else was gone, the oil and the meal remained. Christ — the Spirit, and Christ — the Word, combined to make the cake of truth. Truly, without Him she was destitute. Without Him she could in no wise save herself — only her God could save her.

That special morning when Almanah met the stranger she was looking for two sticks which were hard to find in those days. How strange that Holy Writ should carefully record "two sticks" — just two sticks! Was not the Cross of Jesus made of two sticks? The widow needed fuel to kindle her fire before she died. But wait! What of those two sticks?

What is the significance of these two sticks, or of the Cross? Surely, they speak of a time to come when death will reign over the earth. There will be another woman, the Church, seeking to sustain life in the midst of death. As Almanah, she will be seeking the mercies that flow out from the Cross. Her life will depend upon her finding, not only the Cross, but also the oil — the Holy Spirit. The church will need the sustaining oil from the cruse in order to live through the coming times of famine and death.

Meet the Stranger

While searching for those wondrous two sticks, the Bride will meet the Stranger — the Man from Galilee who promises to come to live and abide with her. He will daily supply her needed oil and meal. Drawing from His provisions every morning, she will prepare an offering — a cake of truth. Daily, this offering will testify to Christ's all-sufficient love and care. Certainly, He must always be served first. And because of His love, God will continuously renew her provisions.

Through His prophet God had promised Almanah, "The rains will not come yet; the famine will continue. But neither you nor your son will waste away. Every morning the meal shall be renewed in your barrel, and the oil, replenished in your cruse. You shall live and not die. And this promise shall be fulfilled 'UNTIL THE RAINS COME.' " And so it came to pass even as the Lord had promised.

Furthermore, God gave her yet another gift — the gift of ministry. Led by God, and hidden away from Israel for many months, Elijah was sent to her house to live until the rains came. He ministered to her and her son, instructing them in the truths of the Lord.

When famine times come to the church, she can be even more enlightened and instructed than in times of abundance. Because of the demanding toil needed to seed and to harvest, the work consumes all the church's energies. Often, during the "busyness" of planting and harvesting, believers cannot find sufficient time to wait before the Lord and listen to His voice.

The rains came as the prophet foretold, and everyone became more than busy making ready for the renewal of life and hope. And when the rains came, Almanah and her son — having been taught by the Lord's prophet — were no longer ignorant as to Jehovah, His ways and His worship. They had been instructed by the Lord as well as sustained by His mercies daily. Almanah who had lost her husband, found life for her son and herself. Jehovah also sent His prophet to be her private minister. The privilege of ministering faith and grace to her own village was given to Almanah. Then, through the Bible narrative she witnesses to the whole world. Her message is: "Faith is the key to victory even in times of deepest adversity."

Open Your Ears to Hear —
Your Heart to Obey

Christ is the head of His church. He is not merely a titular figurehead; He is an active, functioning head. When He speaks to His people, He gives them both direction and orders. Following the Lord's commands will take a believer safely through whatever famine the Lord of the Harvest sends to the once ripened harvest fields.

Do you feel that you or your church are experiencing a time of famine? Is there a scarcity of nourishing bread to satisfy your hunger? Are you like the widow seeking for those two sticks to prepare your last meal? Look unto God.

Hear the words of His true prophets! Do you say, "Where are today's prophets?" If your heart is truly set to worship Jehovah, the Incarnate Christ, your question can be answered. Let your ears be truly open so you can hear the words the Lord will speak to you, for He will send His word *to you* or *send you* to where His word is being spoken. If your ears keenly perceive His words, you will hasten to obey. You will open your heart to the man with the word of God in his lips. In times of famine, God will send His word to enlighten, instruct and direct His church and enable it to move into higher ways of faith, trust, and revelation of Himself.

*In Hebrew, Almanah means widow.

His Gifts Made a Way

In the ancient and beautiful city of David, during the latter days of the kings of Israel, there lived a young man whose name was Dan. These were indeed perilous times. Instability ruled throughout the land because of constant wars — one swiftly followed another in rapid succession. Everyone was frightened and dissatisfied. Food became increasingly scarce and only the very rich had sufficient to eat. The death of King Josiah in battle started the final slide into total defeat.

Rebellious Ones Replaced

When Josiah lost the war with Nechoh, king of Egypt, Nechoh enthroned a puppet king over the people. The new king proved to be so rebellious that the powerful king of Egypt found it necessary to depose and replace him. This became a pattern: one king replaced by another king; one government followed by another. Fear and economic disaster increased until nothing seemed secure any longer. Finally, the rebellions of the puppet kings ended when the mighty Nebuchadnezzar, king of Babylon, conquered Jerusalem.

When Nebuchadnezzar made his final assault against Jerusalem, the lengthy siege was disastrous, and ended in the final fall of Jerusalem. This pagan king from Babylon totally destroyed the city along with its magnificent temple that Solomon had built. He villainously desecrated the temple and ruthlessly carried away all its rich treasures before razing it. During the long siege and the final sacking of the city, many thousands died. Rulers and nobles were slain or taken captive. All the well educated, the handsome young boys and the beautiful maidens were captured and taken into a life of perpetual slavery. Young Dan was one of the fair young men Nebuchadnezzar captured and dragged mercilessly into the cruel bondage of slavery.

For many years, God's true prophets had warned the children of Israel that He was greatly displeased because of their many sins and rebellious ways. Through His prophets, God told them that if they refused to repent and turn back to Him, He would send His judgments upon them. Furthermore, if the people stubbornly refused to humble themselves, and continued to walk in their offensive and provocative idolatries, He would utterly destroy Jerusalem with its magnificent temple.

Tragically, God's words did not pierce the stony ground of His people's hard and obstinate hearts. In their delusion they said, "God would never destroy His beautiful temple!" God called them "a stiff-necked people" because they refused to heed the prophets' warnings. As rebellious children, they set their wills to disregard and disobey the warnings of God's pleading prophets. They preferred to receive the honey-smooth, soothing words of the false prophets of Baal. These false prophets flippantly affirmed: "All is well; all will be well. Seek great things for yourselves; God will not chastise nor reprimand His chosen people." Having turned away from the living God, they lusted after every false idol they set their eyes upon. They continued to descend a precipitous slide into the darkness of witchcraft and worship of devils. Their worship became a debauchery —

an insulting offense to Jehovah, the God who loved them and cared for them. And lamentably, the closer they came to destruction, the more stubbornly they turned away from their Jehovah — so far away, in fact, that they were totally deceived and worshiped God's arch enemy, the devil.

Victims of Rebellion

Dan's parents were among the very few of the ruling class who still believed in Jehovah and worshiped Him. They also believed the words of God's prophets, and carefully prepared their children for the terrible days that lay ahead of them. Dan lived in this tumultuous time of wars. Tragedy, chaos, fear, hunger and sorrow were the companions of his youth in Jerusalem. Crises times had been the pattern of his lifetime. Whenever a brief respite came and everyone thought things would improve, they were suddenly plunged into deeper distress. Members of Dan's family were among the many thousands slain in battle. Frequent were the lamenting cries of the bereaved that pierced the deafening pandemonium and confusion in the besieged city. One person after another surrendered his life to the voracious siege. Many fell victim to stark hunger or to ravishing diseases they were too weak to resist.

Misery, hunger and scarcities; fears, rumors and frightening reports; starving people and countless beggars crowding the streets; dead and lifeless bodies left unburied; a sense of ever-impending doom; hopes of a better future — dashed to the ground; everything constantly deteriorating instead of becoming better; such were the scenes, the memories, the catastrophes which filled young Dan's life.

Fortunately, Dan's family had believed the words of the prophets and turned more and more to God for help in these dangerous and critical times. His parents prepared their children well, praying often with them and, by their own example, teaching them how to pray. In those days, Baal and Molech had replaced the Israelites' own true God — the worship of Jehovah was no longer practiced in His temple. Because in Dan's day it was unpopular to be a worshiper of Jehovah, his family had to worship and pray in the privacy of their home.

Diligently and faithfully Dan's parents strove to educate their young son, not only in the knowledge of their day, but in the true worship of Jehovah. In spite of all the insecurities and blasphemies around them, the family maintained their faith in God. Well did they understand that the anointed prophets were speaking truth — the many sins of God's chosen people had brought these calamities upon them. Dan's family clearly understood that unless God's people turned back to Him in sincerity and obedience, He would bring yet greater judgments and calamities upon them.

The Wounds
of Fulfilled Prophecy

When the true prophets' words were fulfilled, the terrible catastrophes they had prophesied fell inexorably upon the people. Their homes, their families, their cities, and their temples were completely destroyed — their hopes of a better future were utterly shattered. These cataclysmic upheavals brought God's people into the horrors of captivity in Babylon. Along with thousands of other captives, Dan was marched away into slavery, never to see his family or homeland again.

Jerusalem and Solomon's beautiful temple were totally destroyed. Dan's family was killed, his house burned with fire, and Dan himself, now a captive, was branded and forced into slavery for the rest of his life. Any plans he might have envisioned for his future were forever destroyed. For Dan, the slave, there would never be a wife, a home or children. Never would he enjoy the liberty of choosing his own way. He would have no rights of his own, but would be forced to live according to the whims of his masters. He would be at the beck and call of others and would live to please those masters. The perilous times of his youth now climaxed in the restrictive demands of slavery. The conquering minions of Nebuchadnezzar snatched away all that Dan held dear.

Daniel Had a Different Spirit

Under such difficult and demanding circumstances, most people would become hateful, angry, bitter, vengeful and resentful, but Daniel had a different spirit. Adversity — even to such a degree — only deepened his faith, and caused him to lean harder on his God.

Because his family had believed the holy prophets, the terrible events had not taken them by surprise for they had anticipated God's coming judgments. They were not among the deluded ones who believed that these disasters would never happen. Dan had not believed the words of the false prophets who insisted that the idol-gods would never allow God's holy temple to be destroyed. Because Daniel knew beforehand of the calamities — through the prophesies of Jeremiah — he was inwardly prepared for them. He realized that these judgments were God's fulfillment of His promise to visit the people's sins upon them. By faith he understood and accepted the fact that God had fulfilled His purpose: to cleanse Jerusalem from all iniquity with fire and blood. God had kept His word; He did exactly what He had promised to do. This confirmed to Daniel that His God was the one and only true God. Because every word of God had come to pass, Daniel determined that — even in slavery — he would serve Jehovah and trust Him even more during the years of his captivity.

A Refuge in Cruel Captivity

Daniel's faith in the living reality of God's presence in his soul made him outstanding among all the captives. Instead of tragic tears, loud cursings and resentful sullenness, he demonstrated a serene life of faith. He was content with his lot, for he saw God's hand in it. He knew full well that his God was always with him. His troubled spirit could always flee and find refuge from life's many storms in the eternal Jehovah God — his strong fortress. Among the disgruntled captives being marched back to Babylon — into an unknown and threatening future — Daniel's unique calm and peaceful attitude made him a wonder to his captors.

After a long and painful march of nearly a thousand miles, the weary caravan of slaves from Jerusalem finally reached Babylon. Shortly after their arrival, the king ordered his stewards to search out the very finest of the captives — kings' sons, princes of the people, handsome, healthy and highly educated ones. The king separated these chosen youth from the other captives to teach them the language, customs and culture of their new land. Among those selected were Daniel and three other outstanding young slaves. The king planned to supply them with the finest food from his table. After demanding preparations, he would appoint them to an exclusive service — to become servants of royalty.

Jehovah's Rules Recalled

Being wise in Jehovah's laws for good health, and knowing that the king's rich food would make them ill, Daniel and his three friends made a fervent request of the chief steward: "Could we have the privilege of eating our own simple foods rather than the fancy foods of the king?" They were convinced that nutritious foods would make them healthier than the rich foods of the king. The chief steward granted their request conditionally: namely, that after ten days they must appear healthier than the other slaves. Jehovah, whom they served, saw to it that they fulfilled the required condition. After the ten days, their countenance was fairer than the others; therefore, they were never required to eat the unhealthy dainties of the king.

Right Responses Rewarded

Because Daniel and his three friends were wise and worshiped the true Jehovah God — and did not sell out to the idolatries of all their neighbors in Jerusalem — the Lord's favor was upon them. Foreseeing their time of captivity in Babylon, God made His own preparations beforehand. He endowed Daniel with a specific and powerful gift — the ability to understand and interpret dreams and visions.

The young man's peaceful and pleasant attitude made him a favorite with the king. Discovering that Daniel was ten times wiser — and had far more understanding than all the other counsellors, magicians, astrologers and soothsayers — the king made him chief over them all. In fact, the king preferred Daniel and his friends above all the other governmental heads in Babylon.

Because God had a special place and purpose for Daniel, He was continually preparing the way before him. The Sovereign Ruler of the universe had purposed that Daniel should become prime minister and actual ruler over the whole of Nebuchadnezzar's kingdom. Daniel's ascending to the place of rulership would give powerful protection to the Jewish captives. It would also be a witness of their God's mighty power, not only to His own people, but also to Babylon. Even in times of great adversity, Daniel clung tenaciously to his faith in God, and because he realized his complete inability to walk alone, he diligently sought his God daily. In fact, understanding his great need for divine help, he faithfully turned to his Jehovah God three times a day.

An Amazing Dream

One night King Nebuchadnezzar of Babylon was greatly troubled by "a dream of his head upon his bed." Unable to sleep, he arose early, shouting for all his wise men to come immediately. "You wise men," he threatened, "I've dreamed an astounding dream which I can't remember. Either you remember it for me or I'll cut you into pieces and make dunghills of your houses."

Seeing the king so angry terrified the wise men. They knew that they could not do what he was demanding, in spite of all their magic and mysterious wisdom. They began to hedge, to offer excuses, "O Great One, no king ever required such a thing of his wise men! Besides this, wisdom dwells with the gods — and the gods don't dwell with men on earth."

"Stalling! You're just stalling for time," retorted the king, "yours are corrupt and lying words. You're powerless, absolutely powerless! You can do nothing at all to help me." In fiery rage and frustration the king commanded the captain of his guard to do away with all the wise men —

a decree which would include Daniel and his three friends.

When Daniel heard of the desperate king's hasty decree, he went to prayer with his three Hebrew friends. They pled with Jehovah, the God of mercy, to reveal to them the secret of the king's dream and its interpretation lest they also die. God answered their urgent cries.

Jehovah — The Revealer of Secrets

Standing before the king, Daniel declared that he could solve his dilemma, then proceeded to describe the king's dream, and give the correct interpretation. This was Daniel's confident proclamation:

"THE SECRET WHICH THE KING HATH DEMANDED CANNOT THE WISE MEN, THE ASTROLOGERS, THE MAGICIANS, THE SOOTHSAYERS, SHOW UNTO THE KING; BUT THERE IS A GOD IN HEAVEN THAT REVEALETH SECRETS, AND MAKETH KNOWN TO THE KING NEBUCHADNEZZAR WHAT SHALL BE IN THE LATTER DAYS" (Daniel 2:27-28).

What an amazing dream it was! The astounding interpretation made such an impact upon the king that he fell down and worshiped Daniel — a worship which Daniel refused to receive.

"OF A TRUTH IT IS THAT YOUR GOD IS A GOD OF GODS AND A LORD OF KINGS, AND A REVEALER OF SECRETS," said the king to Daniel whose gift from God had persuaded the mighty king Nebuchadnezzar to believe in Jehovah.

Appointed Above All Others

Immediately, the king promoted Daniel, the slave, to the high position of prime minister. Daniel was God's missionary to the king and to the Babylonian people and became a true witness for God throughout the land. Because of his trust in God — and his faithful testimony — he proved that Jehovah, his God, was far above all other gods. Jehovah became honored high above all the idols of that land. The king clearly saw that his so-called "wise men" had miserably failed to help him — to either reveal his dream or to interpret it. The devotees of other gods — the priests, the astrologers, the soothsayers and the magicians — could do absolutely nothing. By his God, this young servant of Jehovah had done what the king required. He proved conclusively that the God-over-all-gods does indeed "dwell with man on the earth."

At once, the king set Daniel over all the governors of the land and over all the wise men, and made him ruler over the whole kingdom of Babylon. As prime minister he sat in the king's gate and governed over all things.

Jehovah Humbled the King

The Lord had determined to destroy idolatry in the hearts and minds of His own people. He would use Daniel not only as a missionary and witness to the Babylonians, but also to His own people who were living in slavery in Babylon. That terrible idolatry, with its wicked practices, caused God to execute judgment upon His own people. Before He would release His people from judgment, He would use slavery to erase and destroy all idolatry.

Because God had much to teach the high-minded, vain, proud, newly believing king, He caused him to dream yet another dream (of a strong tree that was cut down). Again Daniel interpreted it; this time the dream was against the king himself — he would become insane for seven years. This dire prediction came to pass. After seven years of eating grass like the beasts of the field, the king was restored to sanity.

Coming back to his senses after this chastisement upon his prideful nature, the king declared concerning Daniel's God, saying: "I PRAISE AND EXTOL AND HONOR THE KING OF HEAVEN, ALL WHOSE WORKS ARE TRUTH, AND HIS WAYS JUDGMENT: AND THOSE WHO WALK IN PRIDE HE IS ABLE TO ABASE." After learning a bitter lesson of the truth and reality of Jehovah, the king gave a public testimony of his faith in the faithfulness of Jehovah.

The Slaves Dared to Believe

Before the king was driven from his throne, there was yet another test of the power of the idol-deities of Babylon. This time, Daniel's three Hebrew friends would be sorely tested. The exalted ego of the king drove him to make a golden image of himself (similar to the one he had seen in the first dream). He then insisted that everyone, including the prominent people of the city, fall down and worship before the golden image. The king's demand was: "FALL DOWN AND WORSHIP THIS IMAGE OR BE CAST INTO THE FIERY FURNACE!" In this way, he was making a god of himself, and a religion from the imagination of his own egocentric heart.

When the king gave the appointed signal, every man, woman and child fell down to the ground as a sign of worship — that is, everyone but the three Hebrew slaves who insisted on remaining upright. In fury the king threatened them with dire consequences if they refused to worship his image. "WHAT GOD CAN DELIVER YOU OUT OF MY HAND?" he cried. Their faith-filled answer shocked and astounded him, "WE KNOW THAT OUR GOD WHOM WE SERVE IS ABLE TO DELIVER US FROM THE BURNING FIERY FURNACE, AND HE WILL DELIVER US OUT OF YOUR HAND, O KING. BUT IF NOT, BE IT KNOWN UNTO THEE THAT WE WILL NOT SERVE THY GODS NOR WORSHIP THY GOLDEN IMAGE."

When their stinging words of faith pierced the king's ego balloon, his wrath blazed furiously. "Heat the furnace seven times hotter!" the king commanded. Immediately, the king's servants bound the three Hebrew slaves and threw them into the burning fiery furnace. However, because God was with them, they were not harmed; not even a hair of their heads was singed. The only loss they suffered was the burning of their binding ropes. In the midst of the fire a fourth man walked with them — one like the Son of God. Jehovah, the God of the three Hebrew slaves, had come down to walk with them — even in the midst of the fiery furnace.

The True and Living God

This miraculous deliverance astounded the king, and convinced him again of the reality of the God the Hebrews served. Nebuchadnezzar immediately made another decree: "NO MAN OF ANY LANGUAGE OR NATION IS TO BE ALLOWED TO SPEAK A WORD AGAINST THE GOD OF THESE THREE HEBREW SLAVES." Then he added, "No other god can deliver after this sort."

The word of this tremendous miracle of Jehovah — along with the decree of the king — was quickly made known throughout his kingdom. To the people living in the land the king declared, "Jehovah, the God of the Hebrews, is the only true and living God.'' And because of this, many Hebrew slaves turned away from all their former false gods, religions and idolatries. They experienced a true conversion of heart and mind; they returned to the Lord.

Far and wide it was proclaimed that Daniel's Jehovah God was a living reality. Even Nebuchadnezzar, the greatest king in the world of his day, spoke publicly of his faith, and refused to allow anyone to speak against this God, because he was convinced of God's reality.

False Religion Renounced

The king's public stand became a great inspiration to God's people, especially to those slaves brought to Babylon from Jerusalem. After their long time of backsliding from their true religion and worship, and after their multiplied idolatries, they began to turn back to Jehovah — the God of Abraham, Isaac, Jacob and Moses. When the Israelites realized that their God really was the true and only miracle-working God, they finally turned away from their heathen gods who had been unable to save them from captivity. So convincing were God's triumphs in the lives of Daniel, the king, and the three Hebrew slaves that the idolatry and worship of pagan gods was utterly erased from the hearts of the Israelites from that day until now.

Through indisputable proofs, Jehovah convinced the Hebrews once and for all that He was the only true God. By the marvel of Daniel's ability to give prophetic interpretations of dreams . . . by the wonder of the deliverance of the Hebrew slaves from the fiery furnace . . . and by the triumph and the public proclamation of King Nebuchadnezzar's faith in God, Jehovah restored the faith of the children of Israel, and destroyed forever the last vestige of idolatry in Israel.

An Excellent Spirit

Throughout the kingdom it was proclaimed that in Daniel — the young Hebrew slave — there was an *Excellent Spirit*:

Excellent because his faith was strong in His God in spite of calamitous adversity;

Excellent because he believed in the goodness of his God in spite of slavery and the loss of all earthly things;

Excellent because he entertained no bitterness, no hatred towards his captors;

Excellent because of the wisdom that his parents taught him from childhood — that the ways of Jehovah are right and there is no trace of evil in them;

Excellent because God endowed him with a divine gift of understanding spiritual mysteries and interpreting dreams and visions;

Excellent because of his obedience to his captors instead of entertaining anger and rebellion towards them;

Excellent because of his discipline and his complete dependency upon God manifested by his faithful prayer to Him three times a day;

Excellent because the Spirit of the Living God dwelt within his tabernacle of clay.

Not only did Daniel have an excellent spirit in the sight of man, but also in the sight of God who testified of him by the mouth of the angel, saying, "O MAN GREATLY BELOVED, FEAR NOT." And because an excellent spirit was found in him, Daniel was preferred above presidents and princes. Also, because of this excellent spirit, God was able to make him a missionary to all Babylon. As their spiritual guide, Daniel led his own people out of idolatry forever.

And even today, there is a terrible fear and hatred of all idols in the heart of a believing Jew.

Because Daniel had an excellent spirit, God made him a mighty prophet. He enabled him to look far down the corridors of time and to see the mysteries of the future of His people and prophesy of things yet to come.

This is a portrait of Daniel, the man with an excellent spirit — the man "greatly beloved of God":

Daniel — a minister of God and minister of righteousness to kings and princes.

Daniel — a shining light in the gross darkness of the evils of idolatry.

Daniel — who feared his God more than he feared men, princes or kings.

Daniel — the slave with an excellent spirit who became the deliverer and light to his people — who turned them away from spiritual idolatries and back to their Jehovah God.

Daniel — who out of calamitous adversity brought forth tremendous triumph for himself, his people — and even his captors.

Daniel — who refused to eat the bread of self-pity or drink the waters of bitterness.

Daniel — who lifted high his shield of faith and marched through to victory — not as a slave but as a mighty conqueror.

Daniel — who was triumphant in his God, and triumphant because of his faith in his God.

The Stranger Who Embraced
a New God

Moab, a hot fertile land that lay deep in the earth's depression near the eastern side of the Dead Sea, was a harsh land, a land hard to wrest a living from. Inhospitable and very clannish, the people were not given to welcoming strangers. Their religion was idolatrous and their god, Molech (Chemosh by name) was a cruel deity whose worship demanded the sacrifices of children's lives to placate him.

Flee the Famine

Famine had come to Israel. And because of the famine, some families tried to escape its devastation by emigrating to other lands. One of these was a certain family from the area of Bethlehem. This man, together with his wife and two grown sons, emigrated to the valley near Arnon in Moab. Leaving behind their parched, burned lands that the long drought had made barren, they decided to begin a new life there.

Although it took a long time for them to get established, little by little they gained a foothold in the new land. Their economic situation improved; however, Moab never really became "home" to them. The clannish Moabites slowly accepted them (though always with suspicion) because they would not worship their gods and adopt their religion. Nevertheless, this new home was beyond the border of the famine area, and there was always work to do and sufficient bread to eat.

The New Land Has Strange Gods

Because the man's wife was very loyal to Jehovah, the God of Israel, she hated the awful rites of worship of the god Chemosh. Their ceremonies constantly distressed and deeply offended her. Determined to ignore the pagan religious rites that surrounded her, she continued to worship her own beautiful, merciful and forgiving Jehovah. As devotedly as possible she kept His laws of life even in this strange land.

When her two grown sons made friends with two attractive young ladies of the community (and later married them) it brought much sorrow to their mother. Although the young ladies her sons had chosen were pleasant — and she could find little fault with them personally — she ardently hated their awful god. And now, into her own home came the terrible pagan religious rites, for the new daughters-in-law were worshipers of that hateful god, Chemosh.

A Mother's Heart Is Challenged

The mother knew there was only one thing she could do about this situation — pray to her Jehovah for the girls to be converted. Resolving to do everything in her power to teach them about her own God, Jehovah, the mother-in-law determined to win them away from their hateful Chemosh religion. "None of *my* grandchildren will ever be sacrificed to that hateful god in order to placate him or buy some hoped-for blessing,'' she proclaimed. Apart from this false religion, her daughters-in-law were good girls and she was very fond of them. By treating them kindly and helping them, she hoped she could convince them to accept her Jehovah God. He, indeed, was the only true God.

Because this mother's heart and will were set, she took advantage of every available opportunity to tell the girls the wonderful stories of her race and her God. Soon they knew these stories by heart. When she taught them of Moses and Abraham, Noah and Joseph — and explained to them the ancient laws — the girls found that Jehovah's precepts and principles presented a much better way of life than their own religion. As their teacher faithfully shared with them about her merciful, powerful and kind God, they discovered, little by little, that this Jehovah God was much more attractive than their ugly Chemosh. And now, even though they were not altogether certain about all of Jehovah's laws, (given by Moses) they were willing to join their mother-in-law in her times of prayer and devotion.

Death's Sorrow Is Held at Bay

One day tragedy came to their home. Elimelech, the girls' father-in-law died. The sons' wives were truly fond of the older man, for he really had been good to them. He was not as interested in religion as his wife; nevertheless, he was a kindly man, hard-working, and a good father-in-law to them both. His death brought them great sorrow.

At his funeral the girls saw how different their in-law's religion was from their Moabitish customs. They were amazed; they had never attended a funeral like this before! Even in the midst of the sorrow and mourning there shone a strange ray of hope. Although their mother-in-law and their husbands were sad, there was not that desperate, devastating sorrow that always marked death in their Moabitish families. In this new religion, the grave did not become the end of all things.

After Life in Paradise

The family spoke freely of an "after life in paradise" — a place where all their sins were pardoned by Jehovah. Through the rituals taught by Moses, the family had learned of the blood sacrifice on the altar which assured them of Jehovah's forgiveness. Obviously, their husbands also believed in the power of their God to forgive their sins, to take them to paradise to be with their father Abraham, and to await there the resurrection. In their sorrow, it seemed that the family was saying to the departed one, "Good night . . . we will see you in the morning."

Strange customs and teachings these were to the two young daughters-in-law who had never heard such things before, but they liked them. They found them to be much lovelier than the hopelessness their religion provided in times of death. Imagine! How intriguing and encouraging to anticipate another life in a paradise where they would go after death. They were finding the "Jehovah religion" of their new family better all the time. And the faith, courage and hopefulness of their mother-in-law encouraged them to believe that the things they were learning were really true. Never before during agonizing hours of death had they witnessed such sustaining power of faith like they now saw in the bereaved.

In both word and deed, the widowed mother quietly and inexorably brought her daughters-in-law to the place where they were fully convinced that her religion was the only true religion. Concerning Jehovah, they now had no more doubts. They were certain that her God was the true God — that their own god, Chemosh, was both false and hateful. No longer did they worship or participate in the rites of their old temple. No longer could they tolerate the awful dread of its sacrifice and feast days. When the terrible drums would beat, the trumpets blast and the cymbals clash, the girls cringed. How horrible, how shameful, how cruel it was! All that noise to drown out the screams and cries of burning children being offered up alive in the fires to their ugly god Molech. How thankful they were that they had found a better way.

Death Calls Again

Suddenly another terrible day of disaster came to the family. A burning-plague stalked the land. As it was an especially cold winter, many suffered from a high burning fever accompanied by wracking coughs. When anyone came down with this sickness, he just wasted away; no one had any defense against it. The plague baffled the witch-doctors and magicians who worked their charms and canted their spells, but nothing helped. When this dread sickness visited a home, it left few people alive.

It wasn't long before the feared illness came to Elimelech's house. First, the older brother began to suffer the wracking cough and the sad wasting away. Neither tears, prayers, nor medicines could stop it. The youth grew progressively weaker until his spirit fled away from the dreadful torment. Next, scarcely a fortnight later, the sickness struck again — this time the younger brother. The family fought, they prayed, they lived in fear lest it strike someone else in the family. Before a month went by both girls — still childless — were widowed; this double tragedy sorely shook their faith. Could not this powerful God (they had come to know and pray to) have healed their husbands?

Could He not have kept that foul plague away from their dwelling? Was there any god that was true? Or was religion only a human invention to fill up the terrible crater death leaves behind? Death had come and cruelly shattered their lives, their hopes, their dreams; it left in its dreadful wake many tormenting, unanswered questions.

Again they watched their mother-in-law closely: they saw her weep, they saw her mourn, but they saw no devastating doubts or fears enter her heart or mind. In spite of everything that had happened, she still believed in her Jehovah God; her faith had not been shaken. "Sin," she said, "has opened the door to sickness and death, but Jehovah has opened a way through the blood on the altar. There is a door into paradise when we leave this world." When they saw that her faith in Jehovah God was not disturbed — in spite of her unspeakable sorrow — it greatly strengthened the faith of the two young widows. How good to think that their husbands were now in paradise! (However, they wished that their husbands were home again.) How much they missed them! As the empty ache of sorrow refused to leave their hearts, their widowhood weighed even more heavily upon them.

What of the Future?

Added to the fears that came to hound them day and night were these overwhelming sorrows. Unanswerable questions ceaselessly harassed their minds. What were they going to do now? Where could they go for help? The three lonely, helpless widows found themselves with no visible means of support, no work skills and no insurance. What would happen to them in their tomorrows? Because neither of the girls knew which way to turn, their conversations often ended in pessimistic conclusions. And to make things worse, the young widows' families insisted on accusing and blaming them for the loss of their husbands. Had they not made their god, Chemosh, angry when they refused to bow down and serve him? Their "outrageous conduct" and disrespect towards their former god, Molech, had made them hated and feared by their former friends.

In this time of need, no one came to visit the young widows or sympathize with them; no door of opportunity opened before them. They were greatly frightened that their hoarded store of food and coins would soon be gone. What would they do when there was nothing at all left? Instead of holding out a helping hand, the people of their city abandoned them, taunted them and mockingly said, "Both of you are nothing but pariahs — worthless outcasts!"

I Will Return to My People

Finally, their mother-in-law said to them, "Look, not a single door has opened to succor us. We cannot go on like this; I'm going back to my own land and to my own people. At least in my own land I will have friends who will try to help me. There, where I am known among my own people, I shall be able to worship my God without fear, shame or persecution. I'm certain that in Bethlehem-Judah someone will help me; I will not be hated by my neighbors. Surely, I will find a little place and get started all over again. At least, I'll be able to keep body and soul together." And with these words, Naomi, the Israelite from Bethlehem, arose and set her face to return to Israel.

The response of Orpah and Ruth, her two daughters-in-law, greatly surprised her: "Good, we will go with you, for there is nothing left for us here. By adopting your religion, and serving your God, we have lost our place among our own people. No one here wants us! We are only two young and insignificant widows. Our parents have disowned us for marrying out of our race and religion. Our people fear us and say, 'You've brought this calamity upon yourselves! We know that our gods are false and vain and can offer us no help at all. Our husbands now rest in their graves having left us destitute. Our friends hide their faces when they meet us on the streets. Former companions shun us at the well, making all kinds of hateful remarks loud enough for us to hear. What remains here for us? *We will go with you into your land*. Perhaps your Jehovah God will look kindly upon us there.''

So joining Naomi, they sorrowfully prepared their few portable belongings and started early in the morning towards Bethlehem in the land of Judah. At first they traveled silently, for their hearts were heavy with sorrow, and their minds weighed down with thoughts of their bereavement. After all, Moab was the only home they had ever known. Fear relentlessly pursued them as they worried about how they would be received in a strange land, and what the future would bring. Helpless widows they were — and strangers they would be as well. What lay before them in their unknown tomorrows in Bethlehem? Would they be homeless and without friends in this new land? Would they live or die? Tears fell copiously. And the farther they walked, the worse they felt. Hope was, indeed, dim.

My Daughters, Return to Your Childhood Homes

Finally, Naomi spoke, ''Please consider this, my daughters: in Bethlehem I cannot take care of you for I have nothing, not even for myself. I cannot promise you husbands nor can I provide food for you. With faith I return home, trusting that God will open the hearts of my former friends. If not . . . then I will die in my own land. Remember, I've been absent for ten years. Many of my friends and relatives will be gone, and others will have forgotten me. And when I am no longer with you, surely your people will be much more open to you; they will be to you as they once were long ago. Go back, my daughters.

"In time, your families will forget about your marriages into my family, and they will be willing to receive you again. So why don't you both go back home? Even though you have been very good to me — and I have loved you as if you were my own daughters — sickness and death have cruelly raised up a wall to separate us. And what can we do? Return home now, and remember that old Naomi, a stranger in your midst, really loved you. And, surely, you have both loved me and treated me kindly, even as a mother. Go back now to your parents, to your homes, to your friends, to your customs and to your own culture. In Moab you will not be strangers; there you will be accepted."

Naomi's words brought little comfort to the girls who sobbed all the louder and exclaimed, "We will not turn back, we will not turn back!" Speaking quietly, Naomi began to console them and assuage their grief. At the same time, she continued to insist that returning home would be better for them. Indeed, it would be the only sure way for the girls to find security. Whatever the future held, they would be safer in their own hometown than in a strange land where they must face racial prejudice, new customs, a different language and another religion.

Orpah Waivers
From Her First Resolve

After much consideration, the older girl, Orpah, began to waiver. After all, if she apologized most humbly and turned back to that ugly god, Chemosh, surely her people would receive her. As she joined the others in their worship and religious rites, they would once again accept her into their good graces. After all, she thought, she would not really have to believe in this evil god in her heart, for she knew him to be false. Why make waves? If her family and friends believed in this false god, let them believe! And besides, she remembered several eligible young widowers whose wives had died in the plague. Perhaps . . . who knows? . . . surely, something of that nature would not be impossible. Orpah had always been able to get her own way with her parents when she really set her mind to it. Now with Naomi gone and her husband dead, she knew she would be able to return home. Home to her family . . . home to her gods . . . home to her own ways. . . . In but a little while things would again be normal for her. Orpah reasoned in her heart that she would soon forget the past.

When the three women reached the top of yet another hill they stopped to rest. Orpah stood alone and looked back longingly over the way she had come — back to the well-known Moabite lands and fields. She suddenly made her decision. Embracing Naomi — for she had really learned to love this kind mother-in-law and would miss her — she announced her decision to return home to Moab. After all, Naomi could offer nothing, so why should she die in a strange land far from home? Thus, with many tears Orpah turned around and started . . . *DOWN THE PATH THAT WOULD TAKE HER TO HER HOME . . . BACK TO HER GODS . . . BACK TO*

Ruth Pleads,
"Don't Make Me Return!"

As Orpah made her excuses for returning home, Ruth realized that some of the same thoughts had come to her own mind. "Go back to my parents? Yes, I could do that, for they are good people. And with Naomi gone, they would receive me. By appeasing them, I could also regain a place in their hearts. But return to Chemosh? *Never* could I return to that ugly god! No! A thousand times no! Never would I serve him again! Now that I have learned to know and worship the true God, the worship of Chemosh has become utterly repulsive to me."

Ruth reasoned, "Has Naomi not been a light to me in a dark place? Has she not lifted the veil from my eyes and let me see how vile, how unclean, how despicable my former religion is?" The realization that Chemosh worship, so full of evil and darkness, had been birthed in hell was sufficient to dissuade Ruth from any thought of returning home to her parents. Never would she go back to Chemosh! Her mind was made up; she would not return for any reason. To her, a decision to turn back involved far more than just "going home"; it would mean that she would walk out of the blessedness of eternal paradise, and rush back into the hell from which she had already escaped. Ruth chose the sheltering wings of Jehovah — the God who asks so little of us but abundantly pours out upon us everything that we will ever need.

Her conversion and her turning away from Chemosh had truly been complete. Ruth had safely passed the test — the temptation to turn back to security. Her faith in

Jehovah was not merely a mental conviction. Indeed, in her was a deep heart-certainty that Jehovah alone was the true God; His words alone were the true words. She was confident that His ways would lead her into that lovely paradise she had already heard about. Her mind was made up, she would not turn back! She would go to God's land and learn to serve Him rightly. There in His wonderful tabernacle she would worship with the true people of God. There a lamb would be offered up for her sins. There she would know the peace and security that Naomi her mother-in-law had spoken to her of — and demonstrated so clearly in her own life.

Will You Turn Back?

Once again Naomi spoke to Ruth, "Consider, my daughter, that your sister-in-law has already turned back, and slowly worked her way down the hills toward her home. Will you not return with her? Remember, I can offer you nothing. My people are not friendly with the Moabites; in fact, they hate them. The reason that God is angry with your people is because they hired the sorcerer, Balaam, to curse Israel. Fortunately, God would not let him curse Israel, but rather made him bless them.

"Then Balaam evilly counseled Balak (the king of the Moabites), 'on an important feast day, send out your young women to seduce the young Israelite men. Cause them to sin and worship the Baal-gods and Ashtaroth, the goddess of fertility; then God Himself will punish them.' The Moabites followed this evil counsel and tempted the Israelites. Because some of them fell into that temptation, God had to punish them; therefore, God pronounced a curse against your people. As a result, we received specific orders from God not to allow any Moabite to enter our tabernacle to worship with us.

"So go back Ruth, go back now! Although you have gained a real place in my heart — for you are a good girl and I know your conversion is real and sincere — there is no place for you among my people; Israel is no place for a Moabite. But should you feel so inclined, perhaps you can worship Jehovah in your heart even in your own land. Return, my daughter, for I can offer you nothing, *absolutely nothing!*"

As Ruth reflected, she realized that in this new land she would only be known as "the Moabitess." She would be feared and hated for the past deeds done by her forefathers. Let it be so . . . she would go on to Bethlehem just the same. To be a despised Moabitess in the land of Israel would be far better than to be a married woman in good standing in the land of Chemosh. "After all," she said in her heart, "I believe I will be able to earn a living there. And if I die, at least I'll die as a worshiper and believer in the true God, and not as a follower of that false idol of my people." She made her final decision: "I repudiate my own people. I will be an Israelite by choice, by religion, by faith and by living in their land. I will learn their customs and speak their language. No matter what lies ahead, whatever my lot, I will not return. I turn my back upon all that lies behind me, never to look that way again! Family, friends, land, religion . . . they are mine no longer. From this day on they will never again be: *my people, my land, my inheritance, and my gods.* And because they are not the people of the true and living God, I will never return to them."

Ruth's Resolve Dispels
All Her Doubts

"ENTREAT ME NOT TO LEAVE THEE, NOR TO RETURN FROM FOLLOWING AFTER THEE!" she cried, turning to Naomi with tear-filled eyes and a determined look on her face. "Please don't insist on my going back! I've made my decision. There's no use talking any more because my love for you and for your God will not be turned aside by any of your pleadings. For does not the love in your heart for me — that I hear expressed through your voice — contradict the very counsel you are giving me by your words? Naomi, we must go on together for we need each other. You need the strength of my young shoulders, and I need the wisdom of your wise heart. Let us, then, walk on together. . . ."

"FOR WHITHER THOU GOEST, I WILL GO. Just let me follow you! Take any path you wish, go to any village you please and I will go with you. Yours is the right of choice. I will be your maidservant — not your consultant. Yours is the right to give orders, mine the privilege of following them. Wherever you wander, there will I wander with you. If they drive you out from your dwelling, I will flee with you, for I will not be separated from you. Your God brought me peace and hope and life; I choose to remain with you."

"WHERE THOU LODGEST, I WILL LODGE. To me it matters not, Naomi, where our dwelling place will be. A tent? Then there with you in that tent I will be. The slave quarters of some wealthy land owner? I am willing to be a slave with you. My only desire is to be with you wherever you make your dwelling. As a despised Moabitess, as one without any rights, I will take my place at your feet. My only claim, my only cry — let me lodge where you lodge, let me be with you always."

"THY PEOPLE SHALL BE MY PEOPLE. Your people may despise me because I am a Moabitess, but I will not despise them; I shall claim them as my own people, for they are your people. Shall they not become my uncles, my cousins and my kindred? There shall be no other claimant; the welfare of thy people only will I seek. Nor will I strive to profit from them. My only gain will be the honor of being one of the chosen people of God. No unkind treatment of me, a stranger, will hinder me from considering them as my very own family. For being thy family, they shall, indeed, be mine."

"AND THY GOD SHALL BE MY GOD. Well have you taught me to love your wonderful, kind and loving Jehovah. I am determined to have no other god. I hate and repudiate all my former idols; in no way shall they have any place in either my mind or my heart. For me, there is only one Lord, there is only one God, and Him shall I love with all my heart and soul. Naomi, know of a certainty — and let it be engraved upon your heart — that you are not taking a worshiper of Chemosh back with you to Israel. You are taking a fully convinced convert who believes in your Jehovah with all her heart, her soul and her mind, and who has determined to love and worship Him forever."

"WHERE THOU DIEST, I WILL DIE AND THERE WILL I BE BURIED. My purpose is not just to stay with you temporarily (until things get better for either of us), mine is a lifetime commitment. No matter what comes, I will always be at your side. To the best of my ability, I will seek to fill the empty places left by your sons and your husband. You shall not be alone until death itself separates us. Whenever our fare proves to be meager, it shall even then be a shared meal. When wintry winds assail us, we shall both be cold together. In the day that you grow old and infirm, shall I not be your nurse? If the Lord our God should prosper me, shall you not prosper as well?''

"ENTREAT ME NOT TO LEAVE THEE." With these words Naomi stopped trying to persuade Ruth to return. Then the two — one, a weary, middle-aged, heavy-hearted widow, and the other, a pain-matured young widow — continued on the weary three-day journey that yet lay before them. As together they faced the unknown future with its fears and scant fortunes, they looked forward to the coming days with courage and confidence because they were facing them together. Naomi, a true Israelite, was coming home bringing with her a Moabitess desirous of finding a home in her land.

SO THEY TWO WENT ON TOGETHER UNTIL THEY WERE COME TO BETHLEHEM!

From Prison to Glory

Deep in the heart of yesteryear, so long ago that our own land was unknown and our great-great-grandfathers were not yet born, there lived a young man whose friends called him Sammy. Sammy's mother and father were Hebrews; their great-great-grandfather was Dan, a son of Jacob, the grandson of Abraham.

Sammy lived in a time of great trouble, for his people had greatly displeased their God Jehovah by turning to idol worship and the sinful ways of the heathens around them. Nevertheless, in spite of God's indignation and wrath, He still loved His chosen people and determined to bring them back to Himself. He began to turn them back by chastening them for their sin and lifting His protective covering. Now, no longer covered, their terrible enemies the Philistines were able to overcome them in battle and reign over them. These Philistine conquerors were very cruel to their captives and made life unbearable for them. Although the Philistine yoke continually galled the conquered Hebrews, one by one they recognized their guilt, confessed their sins, and repentantly returned to their God. Therefore, Jehovah — ever faithful and merciful — began to work out their deliverance. This is the story of how God destroyed the power of the enemies of His chosen people and brought them once again unto Himself.

A Strange Visitor

About a year before Sammy was born, his mother was sitting alone in a nearby field while his father, Manoah, a very tranquil man, was resting at home. Suddenly, there appeared before her a man with an aspect so strange, so awe-inspiring — yet so beautiful — that Sammy's mother sat silent and spellbound. Speaking with the sweetest voice she had ever heard, he informed her that she would bear a child in the near future. She had never borne a child before and she knew it was now very late in life to have one. Then the man continued, "God has ordained this child to be a Nazarite . . . he must keep the Nazarite vow."

Startled and puzzled, Sammy's mother ran to the house and told her husband what had happened. Who was this stranger? How did he know so much about her? How could he possibly have known that she had no children? How could he predict that she would bear a child in the near future, she having been so many years barren? Was he a prophet? How terrible was his countenance, yet how sweet his voice! He must have meant them good for he brought the promise of their longed-for answer to prayer. The more Manoah and his wife discussed the stranger's words, the more perplexed they became. "This child will be a Nazarite," the man had said. Who were the Nazarites? How long since they had heard anyone say anything about Nazarites!

The Nazarite

Then they remembered that Moses had written about the Nazarite in his third book. A Nazarite was one who made a special vow of consecration to Jehovah — one who separated himself to serve Him exclusively as long as his vow lasted. The Nazarite vowed not to drink any wine or strong drink, and not to cut his hair or beard until the vow terminated. The cutting of his hair or the inadvertent drinking of any wine would violate and terminate his vow; then he would have to begin his vow all over again.

"From birth your child will be consecrated by God to be a Nazarite," the visitor had declared. Therefore, his parents knew that should he ever drink any wine, cut his hair or shave his beard, he would violate this consecration and lose Jehovah's special blessing. As long as he kept the requirements of the Nazarite vow, he could be assured that God was with him in a special way. When he found himself in trouble — at any time, or in any place — he could reach back and feel his long thick hair and know of a surety that his God was with him; His Spirit was resting upon him.

A few days later, this stranger appeared once again to Sammy's mother while she sat in the meadow; this time she quickly ran home and brought her husband back with her. After politely greeting their visitor, Manoah queried him further as to how he wanted them to raise this child that God would give them. Serenely and patiently the visitor repeated to Manoah his former message, giving the same instructions. Not only were there specific instructions for the child, but there were requirements for the mother, as well. As the child must be well born so that he could serve God, she must not eat anything unclean, nor drink any wine or strong drink while carrying him. Manoah then requested permission to confirm this prophesy with a sacrifice and burnt offering to Jehovah. Their visitor graciously gave his consent.

Then to their fearful astonishment, as the flames of the burnt offering ascended, their strange Visitor entered the flames that were burning on the rock-altar, and ascended to heaven. Beholding this marvelous event, Sammy's parents suddenly realized that it had been an Angel of the Lord that had visited them with His message from the throne.

This revelation not only frightened them, but caused them to understand the extreme importance of the child that would be given to them. It never occurred to them to doubt the angel's word — in simplicity of heart they believed.

Sammy Arrives

True to the Angel's promise, the very next year Sammy was born. Great joy filled the hearts of his parents because of this wonderful gift of God to their humble home. Manoah and his wife diligently kept the Angel's instructions — they did not allow wine nor any kind of strong drink in their house lest Sammy might innocently taste it. They simply and fully believed that their son was a special gift from God. As Sammy was to be a Nazarite — man separated unto God — they must, therefore, circumspectly conform to the conditions and restrictions that accompanied such a calling until the child could care for himself.

As a child, Sammy never wearied of hearing the story of his birth. Repeating it over and over again, his parents pointed out what a miracle it was for him to be born so late in their lives. They described in detail the visit of the beautiful Angel from heaven. How wonderful — yet how terrible — was His visage! How sweet His voice! In hushed tones they related that as the Angel left, He entered into the flames burning on the altar. As the fire ascended, the Angel also ascended in the rising flames.

These wonderful stories of his birth created a deep faith in Sammy's heart. In no way did he doubt that he was destined to be special and separated to God during his lifetime. Even when the boys of his neighborhood teased him about his long hair, he was never ashamed of it. For assurance, he only smiled, reached back and felt his long thick hair. Inside he secretly felt really good about it. Because his story was so precious to him, he never told any one; only his mother and father shared this well-kept secret.

Although he did not yet realize what it meant to be a Nazarite and have God always with him, the Angel's promise was very wonderful to Sammy. (Nor did he know the details of how God would use him in the future.) From time to time, however, even as a lad, he sensed the presence of God come upon him and thrill his being.

Philistine Captivity

When Sammy was old enough to understand, he learned that his people were in captivity to the Philistines. Therefore, he soon realized that he must always be careful of what he said or did when some wandering Philistine was in sight. Whenever he saw Philistines coming towards him, he would run out of their way and reach up and touch his long hair; this was enough to abolish all his fears. "Am I not a Nazarite from birth?" he said. "Is not my Jehovah ever with me? Doesn't God have a special mission for me to fulfill?" Sammy knew it was so; therefore, there was no room for doubt. With these thoughts, his courage arose strong within him and overcame all his fears.

Sammy Discovers His Gift

When Sammy was a husky young teenager, he liked to play in a place near a hill where there were many hornets' nests. People called it "Hornet Hill"* and warned all the children about getting too near. One day, when he spied a large hornets' nest in the ground some distance from Hornet Hill, the thought occurred to him to take a big rock and stop up the mouth of the nest. He searched for a rock big enough to completely cover it so the hornets would all starve before they could dig around it. Some distance away, he found a very large stone; now, if he could only move it over to the hornets' nest! Perhaps he could roll it over as it was too big to carry. As he stood contemplating the situation, something strange and wonderful came over him — he had never felt so wonderful before in his whole life. Intense desires to run with all his might, to praise God loudly and to shout with joy, were all jumbled together inside him. In wonderful euphoria, he suddenly picked up that huge rock (which felt like a small toy in his arms) without even thinking what he was doing. Running over to the hornets' nest, he threw down that huge stone which fell with a loud thud and completely covered the hole. "Let me see you dig around that, you ugly stingers!" he shouted merrily at the hornets.

Thinking afterwards about this experience, Sammy wondered what had happened to him. What was this strange and glorious feeling? How could he explain that inimitable sense of exhilaration — that quickening power that almost overwhelmed him as it surged into his being? Was this what the Angel had meant when he told his parents that Jehovah would be with him in a special way? Inwardly pondering what this unusual experience signified, and sharing with no one his wonderful experience, he returned home.

Not many days later, as he wandered out in the hills (several leagues from home) a sudden storm arose. As lightning flashed through the sky and thunder rumbled loudly, rain began to pour down copiously. Knowing he was bound for a soaking, Sammy decided to run home. Suddenly that same wonderful power again came upon him and filled him. He began to run faster than the stormy wind, arriving home before the storm could catch him. "I've never run that fast before!" he thought. "How strange! It seemed like I almost flew across the fields, and arrived home without any breathlessness or feeling of weariness."

From then on, whenever he wanted or needed to do something beyond his natural strength, that same quickening vigor would suddenly spring up within him. Energizing power would rush into his body enabling him to accomplish with ease any task set before him. Sammy realized that this unusual and invigorating power was the fulfillment of the promise — "Jehovah will be with you in a special way." And just as the Angel had promised, this presence came upon him and remained as long as he kept his Nazarite vow and did not cut his hair, take wine nor strong drink.

It wasn't long before Sammy realized that this power was too wonderful to use for "just anything." He must be careful not to displease God by misusing this marvelous gift of the Holy Spirit. He understood, also, that God desired to use this power to deliver his people from the hands of the Philistines. Surely, such power was not for sport or trivial circumstances. Therefore, Sammy looked forward to the time when he could use God's power against the Philistines. Meanwhile, he would keep his hair long and carefully guard his gift.

Sammy Falls in Love

One day the young man met a very pretty young lady who captivated his heart. Yes, Sammy fell in love. He realized he was in trouble because this young lady was a Philistine — one of the hated enemies who treated God's people so brutally, and made life miserable for them in every way possible. These Philistines had cruelly stolen their crops, confiscated all their weapons, and killed anyone who displeased or defied them. But "Philistine or not," Sammy had fallen in love. Being so pretty and so enticing, surely she would not hate the Hebrews like the others of her race.

Completely infatuated with her, he determined to marry her "come what may."

The Roaring Lion

As he had anticipated, his parents were extremely grieved; nevertheless, they yielded to his insistence. According to the custom of the times, a man's parents made the bridal arrangements with the bride's family, so Sammy took his parents to the village where this young lady lived. On the way to her house, suddenly, out from a vineyard like a raging devil charged a roaring lion. His parents froze in total panic expecting any moment to be torn in pieces. But to their amazement, they saw their son, with a strange and determined confidence, face that charging lion with his hands calmly extended as if it were but a small cat. They saw him catch the huge beast, swing him around, and tear him apart as if he were but a tiny goat.

Astonished by their son's incredible exploit, Sammy's parents were stunned. They had always believed that their son was special, but this? . . . From that day on they stood in awe of him. He was no longer "Sammy" to them; he had grown up. Now they called him by his real name: SAMSON — THE SPECIAL MAN-CHILD GIVEN THEM OF GOD. SAMSON, THE DELIVERER OF ISRAEL. How their hearts overflowed with joy and thanksgiving! They no longer worried about this strange wedding, concluding that it must be of God. In some way it would bring about the beginning of their deliverance from the Philistines.

As this unusual episode with the lion spoke to Samson's heart, he mused. "See what lurks and prowls in a vineyard hidden and well concealed but ever ready to catch his prey. Is this why I must never drink any wine, for a roaring lion of evil could destroy my Nazarite-hood? At the same time, is it also a warning from God for me to be careful in my wooing of this maiden?''

Samson's Wedding Feast

On a bright, warm, late summer day Samson walked over to the young lady's village in high spirits. This was the day of his wedding feast. On the way to her house he passed by the carcass of the lion he had slain a few days before. To his surprise, he saw that a swarm of bees had moved in and made a hive which was already well-filled. Removing some of the honey, Samson continued on to the wedding feast eating honey from the lion's carcass. At the feast, it greatly upset him to see thirty young Philistine wedding guests mocking him. How he hated the very sight of them! In anger he proposed a riddle to them offering thirty linen cloaks and thirty garments as the prize. ''I will give you the seven days of this feast to give me an answer, or else you will have to give me the prize. Here's my riddle: *Out of the eater came forth meat, and out of the strong came forth sweetness.*''

The young Philistines pondered three days yet could not find the answer. They grew frightened and angry, for if they lost, it would cost them a pretty penny to give Samson so much booty. Hastily, they went to the bride privately and demanded: ''Get the answer to this riddle from Samson, or we will burn you and your father's house with fire.'' Greatly frightened, she began to entice and plead with Samson saying, ''If you love me, tell me the riddle.'' She made life so miserable for him that finally, the last day of the wedding feast, he told her of the lion he had killed and the honey he had found in its carcass.

When the young Philistines came up with the right answer, Samson was infuriated. He knew that they had not answered it by themselves, but had forced it from his bride. So he went out quickly with great rage to procure for them the prize. As he approached a nearby town, suddenly that same power from God came upon him once again and he walked in and slew the first thirty Philistines he met. Taking from them their linen cloaks and their garments, he brought them to the young wedding guests. Then because he had become so enraged with the lot of them, he left his bride and the guests at the wedding feast and went back home to his parents. Afterwards, his bride's parents, saying nothing to Samson about it, gave her in marriage to one of the Philistine guests who had pretended friendship to Samson.

Samson Catches Three Hundred

After a good while, when his anger had cooled down, he decided to go back and take his wife after all. (This was the time of wheat harvest when much ripe grain was still standing in the fields.) When he arrived at his wife's house, he found that she had been given to his former Philistine friend. When in the fury of this double betrayal, he decided to take immediate vengeance, his belligerent actions opened wide a cause for war. As the power of the Spirit came upon him, he caught three hundred foxes. Tying the foxes' tails together, he set firebrands between the tails, and loosed the foxes into the ripened grain fields of the Philistines.

When the Philistines inquired as to why he had set fire to their harvest fields, Samson told them about his frustrated wedding and his anger against them all. Discovering that he had a cause against his wife's family, the men burned his bride and her family in their house. This grieved Samson greatly. In wrath against them for burning the girl he loved, with God's power upon him he raged through her town and nearby villages and slew every man he could find. Leaving the area, he lived in the cleft place of a great rock called Etam, in the land of Judah.

War Is Declared on Samson

Because of Samson's outrageous actions, the Philistines once again declared war. Gathering an army of three thousand men, they pitched their tents in Judah. Surprised and frightened at this, the men of Judah asked the Philistines why they had come. The Philistines threatened, "If you want to live, go up and get Samson for us. Bring him bound into our camp; otherwise, we will kill all of you."

To the cleft of the rock Etam went the men of Judah to tell Samson the ultimatum of the Philistines. Samson answered, "I will let you bind me and deliver me to them on one condition — that you men of Judah will promise not to rise up against me." When they promised, Samson said, "Now you may bind me with two new ropes and deliver me to them." Immediately, they bound him and took him into the camp of the Philistines.

One Against Three Thousand

How the Philistines shouted with murderous glee when they saw their arch enemy Samson bound in their midst! Angrily they rushed upon him, but ere they reached him, that same mighty power came upon him. He broke his bonds with but a twitch of his wrists. Then, weaponless, he looked around for anything handy with which to fight. Seeing the sun-bleached jawbone of an ass, he seized it and began to slay Philistines right and left as they pressed upon him. The battle continued all that afternoon until not a man of the three thousand remained alive. When God's Spirit and power lifted, he discovered that he was extremely weary and thirsty. Then Jehovah kindly opened up a mountain of water in the jawbone Samson had cast aside; he drank and was refreshed.

This triumphant victory of one unarmed man over three thousand fully armed warriors greatly alarmed the Philistines. Realizing they were doomed as a powerful nation if they did not do something about Samson, they schemed and pondered; they watched and waited; they diligently sought an opportunity to do away with him.

City Gates Dumped on a Hill

Unopposed and unchallenged, Samson walked into one of the Philistine cities. Someone who had seen him enter immediately told the rulers that Samson was in Gaza (the great walled city with massive iron gates for security). Secretly slipping to the gates at night and shutting them tightly, the rulers plotted to take Samson prisoner. When Samson decided to leave late that night, he discovered that the huge gates were securely locked. Giving a sudden laugh of derision, he reached back and touched his hair. Then in quickened faith he took hold of those gate posts and wrenched them from their foundations. Placing posts and gates upon his back, he packed them off to another hill. There he dumped them, leaving the city fathers to discover a way to get them back to the city. Laughing at the joke he had played on his enemies, he headed homeward.

At last the Philistines realized that Samson was too powerful for them. Unless they could find the secret of his superhuman power, they could not possibly overcome him. They finally concluded that he must have power and strength from his God to help him; otherwise, he could never do such impossible exploits. Unless one of them could discover and dismantle Samson's secret power, there would be no use in rising up against him. Surely, it would be foolhardy for anyone to attempt further contests with Samson while God's strength remained with him.

Samson Falls in Love Again

Day and night the frightened Philistines watched him, spying on his every move. When a very beautiful woman happened across his path, lonely Samson once more fell in love, causing the Philistines to think they had a chance for revenge. Spies dutifully reported to the rulers that Samson had often been seen entering the house where beautiful Delilah lived.

Immediately, the great lords of the Philistines called on Delilah. Between offering rich rewards — interspersed with terrible threats — they enticed Delilah to betray Samson into their hands. Having surrendered to their entreaties, Delilah gave herself to the task of betraying her Hebrew lover. Trying every trick she knew — and using all her feminine wiles — she attempted to pry his secret from him by relentless questioning. At first, Samson thought her questions were amusing and played with her by giving false answers. Thinking him serious — and taking his words at face value — she only discovered time after time that he had betrayed her and made her look silly in the eyes of the Philistine lords. This angered and incited her to even greater efforts to discover Samson's secret. Giving him no rest, she began to pout and accuse him of lying to her. Copiously weeping crocodile tears she lamented, ''You don't love me at all; you only lie when you say you love me. If you loved me — like you say you do — you would not hide *any* of your secrets from me!'' Little by little, and ploy after ploy, she skillfully battered down his defenses.

Finally Samson opened his heart to this beautiful, but wicked, traitoress: "From my birth Jehovah chose me to be a Nazarite. I only need to touch my long hair to quicken my faith. This empowers me to do any exploit of strength necessary to overcome my enemies. God raised me up to overcome the enemies of Israel and to set His people free from their yoke of servitude to the Philistines. The secret of my strength lies in keeping my Nazarite vow and in maintaining my long hair. If my hair were cut off, I would be like any other man — I would lose my extraordinary strength."

Betrayed

In deliberate betrayal, Delilah — now realizing that Samson had finally opened his heart to her — immediately called the lords of the Philistines. "Make ready to apprehend him," she commanded. On Samson's next visit she astutely lulled him to sleep. Then, taking a pair of sharp scissors in her hand, she malevolently cut off all his hair. Calling the Philistine lords, she proudly presented her victim, now shorn. When Samson awoke and saw his evil enemies surrounding him, he immediately jumped up to destroy them as before. Then tragically, when he reached back to feel his long hair . . . lo, it was no longer there. "Delilah has betrayed me!" he cried. When he finally realized he had lost his long hair, his faith plummeted to the ground. Samson was helpless before his enemies. Because he had broken his Nazarite vow, the Spirit of God had left him. No longer was he "the mighty Samson," he was just "an ordinary man" — vulnerable and helpless before his enemies.

Samson in Prison

Gleefully binding him and carrying him to prison, the Philistines put out his eyes with a red-hot iron in maniacal torture. Then, yoking him like an ox, they set him to turn the millstone with a long pole. "Hail, you mighty man — you with such vaunted strength; let's see you do the work of an ox!" They taunted and laughed as they lashed his back to make him work faster. Samson was now reduced to toil blindly at the millstones with his prisoner's chains ever clanking with each step. Round and round and round he endlessly struggled.

Samson hung his shorn head in shame. The greatest pain of his humiliating fall was not the lash, the chain, or the agonizing loss of his eyes, but the realization that he had broken his vow and shamed his God. His own choices caused his God to forsake him. Remorse stung his soul like the bites of an entire nest of angry hornets, and this time he had no stone to cover that nest. Grief-filled tears washed from his blinded eyes — like waves from the sea — down over his cheeks. Discouragement scourged his heart with a worse lash than the whip in his jailor's hand. "Why . . . why . . . why did I make such a fool of myself? I knew that Delilah was a Philistine and she wanted to betray me, yet I never thought she would attempt to cut off my hair. Oh, what a miserable fool I was! Why did I trust her? Why did I ever fall for her beauty anyway, knowing that she, a Philistine, hated me, a Hebrew?"

Round and round toiled Samson in his shame and drudgery. Round and round ran the angry self-condemning thoughts in his head. On and on endlessly marched the days of his hopeless, helpless captivity. He — the one who should have been the deliverer of Israel — was now a captive, captured by a pretty traitoress. He — an unconquerable man of war — captured by a woman armed only with a pair of

112

shears! The bitterness of his defeat burned more deeply than the drudgery of his task. If only he had not shared his secret with that she-devil — the secret kept so long to himself! Only God, his parents and he himself knew about the Nazarite vow. Now the enemy knew it well and laughed at both him and his God. Cruel accusations mocked him daily. He could hear the silly songs of the Philistines outside his prison walls as they laughed in glee, mocking him and the power of his Jehovah, the God of Israel.

When Samson heard people laugh at his Jehovah and mock Him, bitterness burned like niter in his soul. He realized their mocking was because he had failed to keep his vows. How could he have done it? How could he have loved a daughter of his implacable enemies? How could he have trusted one he knew hated him in her heart? Countless times a day tormenting questions burned within him. Over and over again he repented, asking pardon for his betrayal. Was not his personal betrayal of God a thousand times worse than Delilah's? She was merely defending her people; he was the fool who defeated God's purposes for his life. God was mocked because of his sin. History would record the story of Samson — the greatest fool in all Israel. God's people would remain in captivity because he had failed. "Oh God, can You . . . will You ever forgive me?" he pled continuously.

Time marched slowly, interminably on. Then one day his captors told him that during the next week they would celebrate an important feast to their god, Dagon. They had decided to exhibit blind Samson to the multitude to prove the power of their Philistine god, Dagon, over Samson's God, Jehovah. This blasphemous mockery — the last and most offensive indignity of his captivity — burned like a hot iron into his already broken heart. Worse than the red-hot iron that blinded his eyes; worse than the lashings he daily suffered; worse than the daily struggle with the millstones;

113

worse even than the chains and shame was the realization that his wonderful God Jehovah would be put to shame before Dagon and the idolatrous heathen. And it was all his fault . . . he alone must take the blame.

Renewed Faith

During the early morning hours of the feast day, Samson was grinding away in his circle of shame. That day, as he toiled, the tickling of his shorn hair on his neck infuriated him. Finally, it became intolerable. Manipulating his chained hands as best he could, he reached up to brush away the bothersome hair. As his manacled hands reached up, his fingers touched the new growth. "HAIR . . . ? Can it be true that my hair has grown again?" he cried in awe. "Yes, it is true!" The impact of this discovery shocked him into remembering again the law of the Nazarite: the Nazarite could begin his vow over again if anything happened to interrupt it. "Oh, my God, can it be true? Can it be that Your mercy will reach such a sinner as I down here in this dungeon? Can forgiveness be my portion after I have so traitorously betrayed You?" His heart melted within him as the wonders of the mercies of God flooded his soul. Again he lifted his manacled hands to touch his hair. Yes, it is true; I know it is true! Have I not felt the annoyance of my hair growing back for some time now?" Nevertheless, the realization of what this meant had not yet reached through to his pain-numbed brain. And now, when he touched his hair, faith sprang up anew in his heart. Now he saw it all so clearly — in the eternal mercies of God, forgiveness had come to him even in his dungeon.

Those wicked Philistines had laid hold of only a part of his secret. That is why they had not realized they must come daily to shave his head to keep his hair from growing again.

They understood not the law concerning the Nazarite. God's eternal truth was that He had been helping Samson all the time of his imprisonment, misery and failure. His Jehovah had heard and answered his prayers; He had brought His gracious forgiveness into his dark dungeon. SAMSON'S HAIR HAD GROWN AGAIN! Faith cascaded like a torrent into his soul. God would give him another chance to release His people from captivity even though he was still blind!

Samson Against Dagon

Samson's fiery faith continued to burn as his Philistine keepers led him into the impressive theater of Dagon where the Philistine's demon-idol sat in all his finery. Even though Samson did not see the blazing light of day, an even greater light now blazed in his heart. Although thousands of the triumphant Philistines came together to see Samson completely humbled, the cheering mob of pagan idolaters only saw Samson standing quietly in their midst.

This Day

"God," Samson prayed, "I ask not for myself. Today I ask You to let me lay down my life for Your people; let me die together with all Your strong enemies who have come to watch my humiliation. Within this heathen temple the great, the strong, the powerful, the rulers are all gathered together. Lord, grant my petition: Let my life be given in forfeit for Your people. Let all these Philistine enemies be destroyed forever in my death. Let them be cast down and completely crushed. Let their god, Dagon, fall. Let not one enemy be left alive who will have the power to torment Your people. Furthermore, let it be known this day,

115

to Your people and to Your enemies, that the everlasting God of Israel is mighty — so mighty that He is able to triumph over His enemies through just one miserable and blind prisoner. Vindicate this day Your glorious name forever. Remember me in Your mercies . . . for in thee do I put my trust.''

In pity a lad took blind Samson up to the massive central pillars that supported the grand temple of Dagon — a masterpiece of architecture. In perfect balance and symmetry these two huge pillars supported the whole structure that could hold thousands in its great hall and balconies. As Samson laid his hands upon those immense columns, suddenly his faith reached up unto God. Once again that glorious power swept through him, filling him with that glorious euphoria. Samson grasped those two enormous pillars — while surrounded by the evil fiends of that god Dagon. He bowed himself in one last mighty effort; the columns buckled under God's mighty power and fell crashing to shattered rubble ere the mocking revelers realized what had happened. ''THE DEAD WHICH HE SLEW AT HIS DEATH, WERE MORE THAN THEY WHICH HE SLEW IN HIS LIFE,'' was Samson's epitaph.

Jesus Greater Than Samson

In some aspects, Samson's life typifies the life of Jesus. Jesus, also, was a Nazarite from his mother's womb. The miracle-working power He manifested on earth was unequalled by men. In every encounter Jesus had with the devil and with the powers of evil, He overcame them and put them to shame. He, too, was betrayed into the hands of His enemies by one whom He counted His friend. Jesus' Father sent Him to be the Deliverer of His people. However, before He had time to set all the captives of Israel free, men bound Him and marched him off to the dungeon under the high priest's palace. How His enemies rejoiced in their apparent triumph as they delivered Him up to the torturers' hands. Nevertheless, in mighty faith and power, Jesus destroyed more of the power and authority of His enemies in His death than in His life. He laid down His life to set His people free. Of Him it was said, "IN HIS DEATH HE DESTROYED HIM WHO HAD THE POWER OF DEATH, EVEN THE DEVIL." Through His death He destroyed all the lords, mighty nobles and minions of that god of flesh, Dagon.

Substance Greater
Than Shadow

As the substance is greater than the shadow, so was Jesus mightier than Samson. Samson uprooted the gates of Gaza, but Jesus tore down the gates of death and bore them away on His own shoulders. They were unbreakable gates of solid brass with bars of iron forged in hell. He carried them far, far away (as far as the east is from the west) till they could never be replaced again. Nevertheless, Jesus was not destroyed in the rubble of those gates; instead, He marched forth triumphantly. Forever free from those walls of the grave, He lives eternally in the power of an endless life. Jesus — the Saviour and Redeemer of Israel, the mighty Deliverer out of Zion — will deliver His people from the hands of their mighty conquerors. Furthermore, He it was who marched in triumph to the gates of heaven and demanded that they, too, open before Him.

"LIFT UP YOUR HEADS, O YE GATES; AND BE YE LIFT UP YE EVERLASTING DOORS; AND THE KING OF GLORY SHALL COME IN. WHO IS THIS KING OF GLORY? THE LORD STRONG

AND MIGHTY, THE LORD MIGHTY IN BAT-
TLE. LIFT UP YOUR HEADS O YE GATES;
EVEN LIFT THEM UP, YE EVERLASTING
DOORS; AND THE KING OF GLORY SHALL
COME IN. WHO IS THIS KING OF GLORY? THE
LORD OF HOSTS, HE IS THE KING OF
GLORY.''

*Zorah means place of hornets.

The Chosen Maiden Chooses

Becky, a young Syrian teenager, was a happy girl, not frivolous, mind you, but a bubbling, cheerful young lady with not an ounce of pessimism in her bones. Born with a merry personality, she always looked on the bright side of life — laughing cheerfully rather than crying pitifully. Her custom was to laugh WITH someone rather than laugh AT them; and when she laughed, others laughed with her. Because she was such good medicine to have around, her friends always welcomed her company.

Becky's rare gifts of sensitivity, empathy, and compassion enabled her to anticipate the needs of others and move quickly to help them. Any suffering she saw in people or animals touched her compassionate heart. Very thoughtful of her friends, she just seemed to know their desires before they expressed them. Her tender-hearted, compassionate nature not only endeared her to all, but made her a delightful visitor.

An Industrious Spirit

Laziness had no place in that Syrian household, for laziness and sloth were luxuries no one in that day could afford — life was truly demanding. She lived in a time when people depended on their own labors to supply their needs.

In Syria the king provided no social handouts to the poor. It was either work hard to put food on your table, or starve; there was no other alternative.

Every morning and evening Becky walked to the village well to draw water, then carried the heavy water pot home nicely balanced on her head. It was a pleasure — not a sacrifice — to go to the well because she loved the excitement and fellowship of the other young ladies of the village who all gathered there at the same time. What fun it was to step down into the alcove of the well's mouth and swing the bucket on a long rope into the cool depths of the well! Even on the hottest days, the well water was always sparkling, clear and refreshing.

When all the girls joined together, how they chattered as they shared the latest news from each friend's home! Then, before filling their water pots for the return trip home, the girls always took cool drinks for themselves. Because they had such fun being together, they did not think themselves wronged for having to carry the heavy water pots on the long dusty walk home. This was their life and their custom; it had always been that way and, supposedly, it would always be that way.

This young lady's forefathers had also endowed her with other gifts: not only was she truly beautiful, but she was healthy and vivacious. She was strikingly beautiful with her shiny raven tresses swept back behind her shoulders; her hair was so long she had to brush it aside when she sat down. Becky's lovely appearance made more than one lad pause to take a second look. Her happy disposition brought a perennial smile to her face; her cheeks were naturally dimpled. Her face, somewhat angular, was pleasingly symmetrical and her teeth, often peeking through smiling lips, were white as fresh fallen snow.

Despite such pleasing qualities, Becky was neither haughty nor vain. Although she was a special child, her wise parents — of whom she was very fond — accepted her as she was. They refused to make any fuss about her being special. She was just their "Becky" — loved, but not spoiled, well-treated, but not pampered, disciplined, but not without wisdom. Her disposition gave her kindness; her disciplines gave her industry. Courteous, gracious and well-trained, Becky was a lovely teenager of her time.

A Decisive Realist

Concerning her unknown future, there was no way she could possibly have foreseen the glorious destiny God had chosen for her, for He had appointed her to fill a unique place in "His story." Because she was a realist, and a very practical young lady, she could not have anticipated what her future would be. Her world was small; therefore, her dreams were small.

Another important facet of this young lady's character was her decisiveness. Once she determined to take a certain course of action, she followed it through. When Becky made a decision, she held to it, not harassing herself with doubts, but steadily worked towards her goal. Fortunately, she was not one to rush into rash and unwise decisions, nor was she stubborn. To be resolute and steadfast, Becky had discovered, made life much easier and more peaceful.

Destiny at the Well

When Becky's "day of destiny" came, she was still in her teens. Not anticipating that anything special would happen that particular day, she continued her normal routine tasks. One daily task she always enjoyed was the evening trip to the well when, with her worn water jug on her

shoulder, she set off to seek water. Little did she know —
that particular evening — the life-changing event that
awaited her at the well.

Approaching the well, she noticed with amazement that
her usually vivacious and talkative companions were
strangely subdued. Quite obviously embarrassed, they were
giggling and looking around curiously. And why were these
ordinarily gregarious young girls acting as though they were
timid? Huddled together at a distance from the well, they
were unsuccessfully trying to hide their giggles by covering their lips with their hands. Perplexed, Becky wondered
as she drew near to them, "Whatever could have happened
to cause this extraordinary behavior?"

When she finally reached the girls, she discovered the
cause of their excitement. Near the well stood a very distinguished looking, middle-aged stranger. He was not alone;
— with him were many servants and ten well-laden camels.
They all looked as though they had just arrived from an extensive journey through the scorching desert. These
strangers . . . Who were they? Where had they come from?
Why had they come? Quite obviously they had just come
in from a long journey for they looked weary and fatigued.
Despite the fact that they were so dusty and bedraggled,
they did not appear to be evil men.

Being neither timid nor fearful, Becky proceeded directly
to the well. Hooking the bucket to the rope, she let it fall
swiftly into the water. Not having to wait her turn at the
well, she was able to fill her water pot quickly with the fresh,
cool water.

Compassion Opens the Door

At this moment, the leader of the caravan approached
her. "Would you give me a drink from your pitcher?" he

politely asked. Cheerfully and obligingly she hurriedly poured out a refreshing drink. Handing it to the stranger she said, "Drink, my lord!" At that moment, the weary camels kneeling nearby drew her attention. "Those camels must be as thirsty as their owner — maybe even more so," she thought to herself. Her tender, considerate heart showed her their need; she moved swiftly to meet it. Without considering what the work of watering ten camels would cost her, she spontaneously and courteously said, "Sir, I will give drink to your camels, also."

As you recall, when Becky promised to do a thing she did it. After emptying the water into the drinking trough for the animals, she ran quickly to draw more. Time after time she ran down into the deep alcove of the well and returned with more water. How the camels drank! Would they ever be satisfied? As those dry beasts hadn't been watered for several days, they guzzled up the water as fast as Becky hauled it out. For a long time she ran back and forth between the well and the trough. Her clothes were drenched with perspiration. Although now looking quite disheveled, she continued determinedly at her self-appointed task. At long last, the thirsty camels were completely satisfied; not one called for more water.

As she was lifting the water pot to her head for the return trip home, the stranger asked her to wait. Then, taking a beautiful golden earring from his cloak and two large, exquisitely carved gold bracelets, he graciously presented them to her. "Who are you, my daughter?" he asked, "and what is the name of your family?" She politely and briefly answered his questions concerning herself and her family. When she had finished, the stranger then spoke of himself: "I am the chief steward of Abraham, your granduncle."

Laban Welcomes the Servant

With the precious golden treasures gleaming on each arm, Becky again hastily lifted her water pot and ran swiftly home. Breathlessly, she told her family what had happened: "I've just met a stranger who was standing at the well. His name is Eliezer and he is the eldest servant of my grand-uncle Abraham."

When her brother, Laban, heard Becky's report and saw the costly golden gifts, he believed everything she told him. He immediately ran to the well to invite Abraham's chief steward to return home with him. As Laban approached the distinguished looking stranger — still standing by the well — he said, "In our home there is plenty of room for you and all your servants, and there is sufficient provender for your camels. Come and stay with us."

When the visitors arrived, Becky's family welcomed them graciously and provided all their needs. Then, fulfilling the common courtesies of that day, they washed the guests' feet, and set a tasty meal before them. Suddenly, Eliezer spoke, "I cannot eat before I tell you why I am here: I've come to fulfill my promise to Abraham."

"My master sent me here to seek a wife for his son, Isaac, who is the son of promise God miraculously gave to Abraham and Sarah. When Abraham was one hundred years old and his wife Sarah, ninety, Isaac was born to them. Isaac, a most remarkably gifted young man, is the only heir of his very wealthy father. Truly, he was God's special and miraculous gift to Abraham and Sarah." Sparing no words, Eliezer informed them of the high position of his master and the wonderful attributes of his son, Isaac.

Words Open New Vistas
to Becky

In much surprise and wonder, the family listened as Eliezer unfolded to them the purpose of his coming. "Abraham delegated to me the responsibility of seeking a wife to be the true help-meet for his son. At first, I felt at a tremendous loss to know how to find this young maiden or even where to search for her. So I prayed to the great God of Abraham and asked Him to lead me to the 'appointed one.' Because I needed a sign from God, I decided to choose a damsel at the well who appeared comely and pleasing, then ask her for a drink of water. If she willingly gave it to me, then also offered — of her own free will — to water my thirsty camels, I would know that she was the one that God had appointed for Isaac."

A Right Spirit Responds

"Anyone observing us would have known how very hot and dry we were, and how much the camels needed watering. I knew that to draw water for the camels would be a very laborious task. Any maiden who would voluntarily offer to do it would have to be thoughtful, compassionate, selfless and industrious. This outstanding act of selflessness would be the sign that this young woman was the one whom Abraham's God had chosen to be Isaac's wife." Then turning to the brother he declared, "Laban, your sister Becky — without knowing anything that I had prayed — has fulfilled every detail I requested as a sign from God." With this, the man ended his story and stood quietly before the family.

As Eliezer, the unexpected visitor, recounted the story of how God had led him, the family listened in amazement.

And the most astonished of them all was Becky who was drinking in each word with rapt attention. She could not understand why her heart burned so within her as he talked. Every word that he spoke about Isaac made an impact upon her. Even though the significance of the man's mission made her blush with wonder, she was thoroughly convinced that this day's events were God's way of answering Eliezer's prayers. Just think of it! She, only a simple village lass, chosen by Abraham's God to be Isaac's wife! The privilege of joining Abraham's divinely favored family as Isaac's wife would be a wonder far above her highest expectations. The little village lass — whose dreams were confined by her village life — was now swept up into the wideness of the eternal purposes of the God of Abraham.

Abraham's Obedience Led to the Unknown

The story of illustrious uncle Abraham, and his call to leave his homeland and family to go out into another country, was well-known. God's calling and dealing with Abraham — and his unquestioning and unwavering obedience to God's Word — had always been a marvel to Becky's family. Abraham, their Abraham, had obediently walked away from his kinsmen (and all the comforts and securities of his homeland) to go blindly into a strange land and into an unknown future. His steadfast faith in the God who had commanded him to go was his only refuge.

Like the fabled "arrows of cupid," the words of Abraham's servant penetrated Rebekah's heart. And even before Eliezer had finished giving all the details of his mission, Becky knew what her choice must be. From deep within sprang a reality of faith such as she had never experienced before. As they were eating, the family questioned Eliezer concerning Abraham, Sarah and Isaac. "What are they like? How did they become so wealthy? What is it like to live in Canaan?" They also expressed many other concerns regarding Becky's future.

Every answer Abraham's steward gave only added more fuel to the fire God had already ignited in Becky's heart. When Eliezer mentioned that he had sworn before the Lord of heaven to find a wife for Isaac from Abraham's own people, Becky's heart rejoiced. Was she not Abraham's grandniece? Abraham had promised Eliezer, "My God will send an angel before you to make everything work out right for you. He will lead you to the right maiden."

The Chosen One

"Why, I am that girl; I'm the chosen one!" Becky thought. "What a wonder that God's angel should seek me out! I know that it was the angel of the Lord who found me, but I don't know why. I'm a nothing — a nobody. Why did the angel choose me?" And even as she pondered and questioned, her faith in Abraham's God increased. Eliezer's words found a resting place in Becky's believing heart. Without knowing anything about the servant's prayer, Becky had fulfilled every condition Eliezer had already set before Abraham's God. How thankful Becky was that she had not listened to the temptation to let him water his own thirsty camels!

New Vistas Demand a Choice

Eliezer addressed Becky's brother directly, "Laban, do you receive what I am saying as from God? Will you and your family answer my prayer and release your sister Rebekah to be Isaac's wife?'' Laban answered, ''This is from the Lord; we cannot say anything either good or bad. Go! Take her with you to become Isaac's wife; we won't stand in the way. We won't resist the purposes of Abraham's great God.''

Commanding his servants to bring in a casket of jewels, Eliezer gave costly gifts to Rebekah and to all her family. To Rebekah he gave embroidered cloth worked with pure golden threads and jewels fit for a princess; and to the whole family he gave other lovely gifts. As a dowry for Isaac's bride, wealthy Abraham had sent many precious and costly treasures with his servant.

As Abraham's son, Isaac would inherit everything. His inheritance included not only his father's wealth, but also the precious promises God had given to Abraham. One of these promises was that Abraham would bring forth seed for many generations to come. Remembering this, Becky realized with much joy that when she became Isaac's wife, she would also share his glorious inheritance.

Becky's Choice

The next morning when Eliezer said, ''Send me away with Rebekah; I must return home to my master,'' the family cried, ''No! What's the hurry? Let our sister stay with us for at least ten days more, then we'll let her go. These few days with us will give her time to become accustomed to the shock of leaving us. Your land is over a thousand miles away; surely, it will take you at least fifty days to reach your home. And because we'll never see our happy sister again, you must allow us time to get adjusted to her going so far away.''

But Eliezer, being a very wise man, did not want to give the family time to try to persuade Rebekah otherwise. He must not let them work on her sympathies, appeal to her family loyalties, or scare her with comments about the weariness and dangers of the extended journey. "If I tarry here ten days," he deliberated, "and her family continues to assail her with their barrage of fears and doubts, they might succeed in dissuading her from going. When her faith and hope are tested, and the wonder of the expensive gifts has faded, will I lose my prize?"

"We Must Go Now!"

Having decided what he should do, Eliezer emphatically declared, "No! I must travel immediately." The family's spontaneous response was to continue protesting, "You haven't given us time to prepare; this hasty decision is too much for us. Please give us a few more days." And then finally, "Well . . . let's call Becky and let her answer for herself."

When Rebekah arrived at the family counsel, she found her mother in tears and the whole family silent and morose. They acted as if a most precious treasure was being ruthlessly snatched away from them. Suddenly, her brother Laban stood up. Looking at Becky intently, he asked the crucial question, "Wilt thou go with this man?" Becky had already made her decision.

"Wilt thou go with this man?" Laban repeated. "Will you leave your own kindred? Will you risk your life on such a dangerous journey? Do you believe that what this man has said to us is true? Will you risk your future happiness to go on a perilous journey across wild deserts, with only the promise of finding a wealthy husband? Have you not already found someone pleasing to you right here in your own land, in your own village? Are your ties with your family so weak that you can leave us without further thought?

Will you go with this man because he said a prayer and you unwittingly answered it? Can you trust yourself in the hands of this stranger who has no other proof of his good intentions than his prayer and these costly gifts? Rebekah, answer us, WILT THOU GO WITH THIS MAN?''

Rebekah's Faith and
Determination Triumph

Out of the reality of a newfound faith, Rebekah determined to stand by her decision and not be shaken. Her determined heart and her very nature inclined her to stand by her word. This man's testimony had brought her certainty and deep assurance. Now she knew in her heart that God had prepared her from the womb for this place. As Isaac's wife, this happy child of destiny would give her family an answer that would sound forth that day and ring throughout history.

With sincerity and serenity, yet without hesitation, Becky spoke those fateful words, ''I WILL GO! . . . Yes, I'll go with this man. I know that the great God of Abraham has sent for me to join my life with Isaac's. I know that I'm the answer to this man's prayer for a sign. (I wondered at my willingness to work so hard as I watered all those thirsty camels!) Although I had no idea that the strangers were from my granduncle's house, I just knew that I had to water the camels; I knew it was right. I fear not the long and arduous journey, for the God of Abraham shall go with me. I go with the certainty in my heart that this is my destiny — this is my life! Farewell, loved ones, home, mother, friends and possessions. Yes, and gods. From now on the God of Abraham shall be my God, also.''

Her answer, ''I WILL GO!'' continues to ring down the corridors of history. That decision caused her to become one of the favored progenitors of the great "SON" yet to be born — the only begotten Son of the eternal Father.

When Becky said that she would go, her family could not alter her decision by either entreaty or argument. And because she chose to go, that very day she made all the necessary preparations. Willing to leave behind everything dear to her, she joined Eliezer's caravan, ready to set out into the unknown future, never to return to her home again. With only Eliezer as her guide, she eagerly left her homeland. A tedious and rigorous journey lay before her — of that she was certain. But she also knew that it would lead her to her beloved. When the difficulties of the long journey through the desert were over, she knew that Isaac would be waiting for her. Nothing else mattered. Lifting her eyes to the far away land, she departed, trusting in the God of Abraham to soon unite her to the one He had appointed for her.

"Wilt Thou Be My Bride?"

Looking through the window of this story and contemplating the intriguing romance, a wondrous glory is seen — a glimpse into eternity. This story, so rich in detail, paints a picture of a strange and unusual courtship instigated by the Lord Himself. Surely He recorded it in Sacred Writ to reveal something far deeper and more meaningful.

There is another romance, another Father, another Son, and another Bride who live in a far off country. There is another Servant — the Holy Spirit — the One sent to be our Comforter and Advocate. He is the One who now stands at the Wells of Salvation waiting for those who will come for the *water of life*. The Holy Spirit came seeking for the God-chosen ones to prepare them to become the Bride of His eternal Son. These are the ones who will give themselves voluntarily and wholeheartedly to love the Lord Jesus Christ and to serve Him with all their heart and strength.

This Servant waits at Salvation's Wells to see who will come to draw water, and who will offer Him a drink. He awaits those who are willing — not only to minister to Him — but to serve His companions as well. This Servant wants to reveal, in His own inimitable way, the glories, the riches, *the greatness of the Father and His only Son who is the sole heir of the Father.*

As Rebekah, can you also hear the tempter saying to you: "What is the hurry? Stay around awhile until you are sure. Don't make such a final and total commitment. Think what it will cost you! Consider all that is involved: the dangers, the unpleasantness, the perils of following this servant off into the wild and demanding desert. Are you truly willing to embrace God's binding promises for your life? Stay awhile. Tarry with me yet another seven years in my land." Have you asked yourself why the Servant is in such a hurry? He wants to go *now!* He doesn't want to give the tempter time to alter your decision. Consider well, then tell me — "WILL YOU GO WITH THIS MAN?"

Is Your Answer, "I Will Go"?

There are those who have found the Pearl of Great Price — the love of their hearts — those who have already sold all to possess it. They have already fallen in love with Him — the One whom having not seen, they love. Such ones are careful not to give answer to the ever-pleading tempter or to be troubled about the material things they have left behind. Simply and unequivocally, the answer rings forth from the devoted hearts of those who have already made the commitment. Binding bracelets of divine apprehension have already been placed upon their wrists. "I WILL GO!"

they shout. And beyond any retraction, these words ring forth into all eternity from each heart: "I will cross any barren desert — no matter how long the journey may be — because I know that I shall soon meet my Heavenly Isaac. That alone will suffice me! Farewell, world . . . friends . . . possessions. Farewell, idols and pleasures of this world. As a bride, I go out to meet the Son of the everlasting Father, even Isaac!"

The Sinner
Discovers Worship

What excitement rippled through the city that day as people chattered the exciting tidings from roof top to roof top. Across backyard fences and at the town well everyone was busily exchanging the shocking news: "Have you heard? Did you know that Simon the Pharisee invited Jesus to have dinner at His house . . . and that Jesus accepted his invitation?" The villagers talked on . . . "Will wonders never cease? That rich Pharisee inviting Jesus! Why would Jesus — of all people — go to visit someone with Simon's religious reputation? Didn't He know that Simon certainly was not his friend — that he frequently talked calumniously against Him? Jesus *must* have known the terrible things Simon had said about Him to the townspeople."

The people questioned ceaselessly: "Why was Jesus being friendly with a Pharisee? Did He expect to befriend him? If Jesus could make a friend of a Pharisee, it really *would* be a miracle. By accepting Simon's invitation, was Jesus attempting to break down some of the prejudice and hatred of the Pharisees towards Him? And what hypocritical intrigue was the Pharisee up to now? Surely, concerning Jesus, it was certain that Simon desired no good. Or was this just a political ploy to 'make points' with the Sanhedrin? Would Simon seek to entrap Jesus in their conversation?" The villagers speculated many things about this coming event. But whatever may have been Simon's reasons for the invitation, Jesus had promised to come to their town that day! Whatever the speculations and conjectures of the townspeople were, this news was exciting.

I Will See Him!

Early in the morning many people crowded alongside the roads to see Jesus and His disciples as they entered the town. The people had lined up as though waiting for a parade. There was one, however, who did not join the others at the roadside. Her absence was due to the fact that she was even more involved with His visit than the waiting crowds. Everything that she had heard about Jesus — this unusual, miracle-working young man — had made a deep and lasting impact upon her heart. As she considered His coming visit, she determined to attend Simon's dinner. The fact that she had not received an invitation didn't bother her; she would go, uninvited. "I *will* go; I *will* see Jesus for myself. I know that Simon will let me come without protest," she smirked to herself, "I anticipate no trouble at his door."

In the town there was, in fact, much discreet whispering concerning this beautiful young lady. Rumors abounded, but they were whispered softly lest the wrong ones should hear, for one could get into trouble if too careless with his tongue concerning Simon the Pharisee. How friendly she was with Simon! How often she visited his home on one pretext or another, and how well she was always received! The whisperers said she had been seen slipping out of his home late one dark night all by herself. Sly rumors pointed out that when she met Simon on the street, they both were very friendly with their greetings. But because nothing, absolutely nothing, was ever proved, the people kept on wondering and the people kept on whispering — as people always do.

135

He Will Surely Notice Me

However, this day would be different: she was not paying Simon a visit, she was going to see Jesus. After painting her face with a most delicate touch (not too much, mind you, but just enough to make her appear fresh and attractive), she adeptly painted her eyes accenting their striking, deep-brown brightness. Calling in her favorite hair dresser, she asked her to skillfully fashion her beautifully long hair — so luxuriant and glistening. She wanted it to be noticed. "I must really make a good impression on this young man," she mused. "All young men look at me. Jesus will certainly look at me with admiration, too. No doubt He will take time to talk with me alone. Should I take Him a gift? What shall it be? Ah, I know, my favorite spikenard — so expensive and impressive. When He recognizes me, I will casually hand the ointment to Him. By then, He will pay attention to me, talk with me and answer some of my many questions. Maybe He can answer some of the enigmas that perplex me . . . the reality of heaven and hell, and matters concerning sin and righteousness. For I must confess that I am quite troubled at times about these things, especially when I think of . . . Ugh . . . Death!"

Then her light young heart began to think of some of the religious questions she would ask to impress Him with her knowledge of religious values. Perhaps He would explain how He performed some of those miracles she had heard about. "Would He possibly pay more attention to me than to Simon? Ha! Wouldn't that make Simon jealous!" And then she laughed. After all, the old fool couldn't really say anything against her — they both had a secret that he dared not expose. In fact, that secret was quite lucrative to her and kept her in the style in which she delighted to live. Fate had been good to her, giving her such beauty and making her so admirable to look at.

Now, while she was still making herself pretty, Jesus had already arrived at Simon's home. Her servant ran to tell her that He was already there, and would soon be invited into the dining room. Hurriedly, throwing her velvet cape about her shoulders, she went to visit Jesus at Simon's house. She knocked, then marched right on in. No one detained her at the door, for Simon's servants had standing orders concerning her. As the attractive young woman entered the dining room she saw Jesus reclining on the couch ready for the banquet.

Honored Guest Neither Welcomed Nor Accepted

Simon's careless manner of receiving Jesus in his home let Him know that His host neither considered Him a friend nor did he respect Him as an honored guest. By offering none of the common courtesies that custom afforded to special guests, Simon's discourteous treatment clearly informed Jesus that the atmosphere — if not hostile — would definitely not be friendly. By having Jesus as his guest, Simon was probably making some political maneuver. Whatever his motive, this proud Pharisee expressed loudly and clearly that he did not consider Jesus an esteemed guest in his home.

Ignored and Annoyed

The bright, well-dressed, young woman had walked into the dining room with a comfortable air about her as if she belonged there. With His back towards her, Jesus was courteously conversing with Simon, and did not turn to acknowledge her presence. Seeing her, Simon blanched with trepidation, but said nothing. Her discreet coughing a few times failed to distract Jesus from His conversation with Simon. Perplexed, she just stood there wondering what move she should make next to gain His attention and proceed with her programmed interruption.

Ignored, Yet She
Was Attentive

Something was wrong. Things were not working out as she had planned. The fact that Jesus ignored her vexed her greatly. His disregard for her presence continued for what seemed to her an interminable time. Standing behind Him as He reclined on the couch, she listened to His calm sweet voice. And as she listened, she felt the intense cadence of His voice penetrate her inner being. She began to experience something indescribable, flow through her — something uncomfortable yet sweet. Something painful yet lovely. As her eyes turned inward, she began to see herself in a new light. Her once well-hardened conscience began to smite her with agonizing blows. Oh, that somehow she could flee and hide from the light that was entering her soul! Strangely, yet imperceptibly, she was aware of being transported into a holy place, holier than the very synagogue of her town. And as she stood in that holy place, unclean and leprous, she felt more miserable by the minute. What could she do? How could she escape? It seemed as though the very world stood still — as though she already was standing undone, ashamed and frightened before the high and holy tribunal of God.

Ignored, Yet She Responded

Unbidden, a fountain of tears that had not been awakened since her childhood began to spring up and flow copiously from inner hidden rivers. Like a cascading river in spate, tears poured out beyond her control. Down her cheeks the hot, impatient tears streamed, and then splashed gently upon Jesus' feet as He reclined on the dining couch before her. They refused to stop; they just silently flowed on and on as they bathed His feet. An unquenchable river opened within her; her whole inner being was quickly slipping out of her control. Feelings, emotions, thoughts — unwanted and unbidden — took control of her soul and mind; suddenly, shame brought her composure into ruins. Her carefully applied make-up streaked down her face and stained Jesus' feet. And strangely to say, He apparently had not even noticed it nor paid any attention to her whatsoever. Jesus failed to look at her or speak to her. "Simon will probably be furious with me for crying and looking like a shrew in his house," she thought.

Jesus did not seem to notice her . . . but Simon would have murdered her right there (if looks could kill). Fortunately, his look of rage didn't bother her at all. By now, her inner world had captured her every thought, and she did not even care what anyone thought about her or her actions. Seemingly unperturbed by all that was taking place around Him, Jesus kept on talking to Simon, evidently paying no attention to her. In fact, Jesus had not yet even looked at her.

In His Presence
Truth Is Disclosed

By now, her desire to make a good impression upon Him had disappeared. Her carefully thought-out plan of presenting Him with her gift — and thereby buying His good will and favor — was forgotten. No longer boasting and gloating in an exalted opinion of herself, she now saw how utterly black and sinful she truly was. Totally devastated by the realization of how evil and ugly she was within, she saw her shapely body only as a prison for her mean and filthy heart — a heart that was now loathsome to her. How desperately she longed to be able to escape from the blackness within! How she yearned for a new chance to begin life all over again! How different life would be if she could only change all the past! As conviction pierced her heart, and deep repentance gripped her soul, she inwardly cried, "How utterly unworthy of either mercy or forgiveness I am! Oh, that some ray of hope might enter the darkness of my night of damning sin!"

Shame Awakens a Stony Heart

As she pondered the dreadful condition of her heart, the tears would not stop flowing. "Oh, for a lamb to slay at some altar," she exclaimed, "where I might find relief for this ugly stain upon my soul. Oh, for a priest to absolve me from my evil ways — for a mediator who would stand between me and a holy and offended God! Oh, that in some way I might be like this Jesus: so pure, so holy!" Before being in His presence, she had not realized that He was so holy. How did she know Jesus was so holy? She could not tell how she knew . . . she just knew it was so. With deep shame, she remembered how she had planned to entice Him with her charms. How fortunate she was that He had paid her no attention at all.

At His Feet I Fall

Looking through tear-dimmed eyes, she realized that His feet — still soiled by the grime of the dusty road — were now also stained from her make-up. Suddenly, something inexplicable broke within, and with the pain of a broken heart and the groan of a crushed spirit, she softly sank down on the floor behind Him. Powerful forces continued to surge within her and overcome her ability to maintain control over her feelings and emotions. Her tears bathed Jesus' feet.

Unfastening her beautifully coiffed hair, she used it as a towel to dry His tear-cleansed feet. What did it matter now how soiled her hair had become, she could wash it later. Her looks no longer mattered. The ugliness outside only reflected the truth of her inner being — so ugly and vile.

Drying His feet with her luxuriant hair, she felt an overwhelming desire to kiss His feet without restraint. How strangely different she now felt than when she had first entered the house! These were not the kind of kisses she was accustomed to; somehow they came from an inner well of longing and affection. She had never experienced this before. Her kisses were so pure and so deep; they sprang from a well of total surrender — a surrender that comes only with complete abandonment and deep love. No matter what Jesus might ask her to do, she knew that from now on she would love and obey Him with all her heart.

With absolute certainty, she realized she was not in the presence of a man; she was in the very presence of God. Jesus was not just another young man (as she had formerly imagined); He was God dwelling in flesh. A love so pure and holy arose within her that she wondered as to its precious source. Certainly it was not like any other love she had ever experienced before. In that moment, she determined to never again return to her old life — she would become a disciple of this holy Jesus. Now her heart understood that all the things His disciples said of Jesus were true. They had proclaimed that He was their long awaited Messiah — their God come down from heaven to visit them. And she believed their every word. Join them she would, and become one of Jesus' disciples. It would have to be in secret, for He would never have one in His company who was as vile and sinful as she. Her desire for riches had utterly vanished. What a high price she had paid for such filthy gold! Never again would she visit this house of shameful memories. In an eternal moment, her heart pledged to love and worship this Christ till the very end of her days. She knew that she would never again return to the bondage and customs of her old life.

The Sweet Fragrance
of Surrender

After drying His feet and wiping them clean, she noticed her flask of spikenard laying nearby where it had fallen. Grasping it and breaking it open, she poured its sweet fragrance over His feet. And even as she anointed His feet with the oil, she somehow felt that He was not offended with her. How could it be that Jesus still did not seem to be aware of what she was doing? As the sweet odor of the fragrant spikenard filled the air, she felt a deep peace steal over her spirit.

Her thoughts returned to the time when she was a little child and had sat quietly at her father's feet. How these precious times with him had stilled her fears, quieted her questions, and made her know that everything would be all right. Yes, long before she went down that terrible road of rebellion and degradation that so ruined her life, she had enjoyed a father's love. That was before her father had been killed and she had opened her heart to those contemptible rebellions against society and against God. There at Jesus' feet she understood so clearly what a ruin her life truly was — what a fool she had been! And now, prostrate before Him, the realization of what chaos and ruin her rebellions had brought into her life overwhelmed her.

Recognition for
Humble Service

As though entranced, she continued to kiss Jesus' feet; it seemed like she could not move — nor did she desire to. Would that she could stay there forever in the pure delight that flooded her soul! Suddenly, as if in a dream, she heard Jesus' words; He was chiding Simon for not receiving a guest with the common rites of courtesy. "Simon, I came to your house, but you brought no water to wash my feet. You received me with no kiss of welcome. You offered no fragrant oils to anoint my feet." Immediately, she snapped out of her reverie when she realized He was talking about her.

"SEEST THOU THIS WOMAN? SHE HATH WASHED MY FEET WITH TEARS AND WIPED THEM WITH THE HAIRS OF HER HEAD," Jesus said. "Is Jesus talking about me?" she wondered. "Yes, I did wash His feet with my tears — and I didn't even think He had noticed! It's true, that's just what I did." After all, Jesus had been aware of everything she was doing. The realization that He had really noticed her made her want to hide her dirty tresses, now no longer shiny and beautiful. "How humiliated I am . . . but after all, does it really matter now?" she thought.

"BUT THIS WOMAN, SINCE THE TIME I CAME IN, HAS NOT CEASED TO KISS MY FEET," Jesus continued. "Will Jesus be offended and angry with me?" she wondered. "I just couldn't help it; love for Him overwhelmed me. I hope He doesn't scold me here in front of everybody; I'm ashamed enough just being in this house. I never want to see Simon's shameful place again."

" . . . BUT THIS WOMAN HAS ANOINTED MY FEET WITH OINTMENT," Jesus was saying. "Will He be pleased?" she questioned. "I hope so. Or did my actions make Him angry? If He would only look at me, then I could see if He was angry." She felt like a captive, afraid to move lest at any moment something might destroy this tenuous delight she was experiencing as she anointed His feet and kissed them.

His Piercing Eyes
Penetrate Her Heart

Still speaking to Simon, Jesus now turned to the woman and looked upon her with mercy and compassion. As His eyes pierced into her inmost soul, He immediately saw everything within her. From those piercing eyes nothing could be hidden. In His look she saw a depth of love and compassion beyond anything she had ever known. And His love annihilated and swept away the fear she would have otherwise felt. Compassion and mercy, love so pure, so deep, and selfless — yet so knowing — met her eyes, and immersed her in an ocean of grace. She felt so humble and repentant, yet so clean and so loved. How could she explain this mystery that flooded her soul?

But wait, what was Jesus saying? "HER SINS WHICH ARE MANY. . . ." "My Lord, how true that is," she reflected, "my sins *are* so many, so vile, so terrible. . . . Now that I love Him, how ashamed I am of all my transgressions!"

"HER SINS WHICH ARE MANY," Jesus had said, "ARE FORGIVEN, FOR SHE LOVED MUCH." "What? YOU MEAN MY SINS ARE FORGIVEN?" she said breathlessly. "Have I heard right? My Lord and my God, are my sins truly forgiven?" Joy flooded through her soul as He said to her, "Yes, I am speaking to you."

"THY FAITH HATH SAVED THEE . . . GO IN PEACE." "Oh, my Lord, can such mercy be mine?" she questioned. "Can such grace be poured upon me? I have come to love You, Jesus, but I will love You a thousand times more, for You have been gracious to me — a sinner."

Released and Cleansed

Into her conscience came a rest, a glory she had never experienced before. Christ's words produced within her a deep feeling of being totally cleansed from all her sin. She could now stand in front of Jesus' piercing eyes and know that she was clean deep within her soul and spirit. No longer did she need to be ashamed nor hide, because she had found a refuge right here in her beloved Lord. With a faith born of love, she laid hold of Christ's glorious, creative words and knew that she would never, never be the same again. Now she was a new woman — her whole life had completely changed. She determined to be Jesus' disciple for the rest of her life.

The Captive Set Free

Christ dismissed her saying, "Go, but go in peace." On winged feet that did not seem to touch the earth, she turned to leave that household forever. Behind her she left its secrets and its shame. She was free, oh, so free! Peace, PEACE — like the calm after a violent storm — arose within her. And joy, JOY — like a bubbling fountain sprang up within her heart inundating her soul. And love, LOVE — far beyond the love which she had always wanted (yet could never find) — filled her. She knew that for all eternity she was forever in love with Jesus the Nazarene, her Lord and her God.

She wanted to sing; she wanted to dance through the village streets, even with her grimy hair flying in the wind. She wanted to shout at the top of her voice as she realized the glorious wonder she had experienced. No longer was she a sinner — she was clean! When He washed her by His creative word, she became a new creature. The villagers — who saw her bounding like a frisky colt escaped from its stall — wondered what in the world had happened to her. As they observed her singing and dancing, one said to another, "Could this possibly be that Mary from Magdala?"

Obedience Unto Sacrifice

Out of the awesome blue of the sky above came those life-shattering words to Abraham, "Take now thy son, thine only son Isaac, whom thou lovest, and get thee into the land of Moriah; and offer him there for a burnt offering upon one of the mountains which I will tell thee of."

This was Abraham — the man of amazing faith. There were no Scriptures to help and guide him, nor were there examples of men of God to inspire and confirm his beliefs. His determined faith was in God, the living God, who had spoken to him only seven times before. His faith in God brought him into obedience. Each time God came and spoke to him, Abraham's works validated his faith.

God's voice he could never mistake; it had been the guiding light of his life and had thrilled and blessed him. Yes, Abraham knew well the voice of his God; he knew it with such certainty that he could not doubt it. That voice entered — not only into his ears — but penetrated his whole being with divine reverberations.

God's Words Reveal His Unsearchable Ways

Now, for the eighth time, God's voice comes again to Abraham with words that seem to contradict and invalidate the promises already given: "In Isaac shall thy seed be called." Before, God had told Abraham that this son, Isaac — born so miraculously by his wife, Sarah — would be the father of many nations. His progeny would be as numerous as the stars in heaven. Thus far, all that God had spoken to him had come to pass — the amazing miracle happened and the promised child was born. At Abraham's side stood his beloved miracle-child, the wonder of his whole household, the fulfillment of God's promise — the certainty of the great nation to come.

Now again, God's voice (that he could not mistake and would not doubt) came to Abraham telling him to slay Isaac and to offer him up as a burnt offering. How could this be? Isaac was not yet married, nor had he brought forth any children upon the earth. How then could God keep His former promises? Was this truly his God speaking to him now with such shattering and seemingly contradictory directions? This voice that he was now hearing . . . was it the same precious voice that had spoken to him before? Or had he mistaken the voice of the devil for the voice of God? Was he somehow being deceived? Could this benign God — who had been so kind and good to him through the years — now desire to slay the son of His promise? Could his God have such a blood-thirsty, cruel nature? Could it be that he was hallucinating and this was not really God's voice he was hearing? Abraham wondered.

Obedience —
An Established Pattern

All through the years, Abraham had obeyed the voice of his God, and because he really knew that voice, it was not going to be any different now; he had made up his mind. "My God is good! He cannot, and will not do any evil; nor can He lie. In someway, God will surely make this strange command turn out right. His promises will all prove to be true. My God is a miracle-working God; the birth of Isaac amply proved that." Abraham had established an irrevocable pact with God: when God spoke, then he *must* and *would* obey His voice; he would not question either God or His ways. God had again spoken — of that Abraham was certain — he must obey.

Isaac was a very loved child, a miracle child; he was their child of promise, their child of destiny. There were many strong factors in Abraham's heart that made Isaac especially dear to him. Knowing Abraham's deep love and devotion for Isaac, God — who moves in mysterious and unsearchable ways — made this demand upon Abraham's faith and obedience. In effect, God said to Abraham, "Do you love Me more than you love your beloved son, Isaac? Do you truly love Me more than all My works, My promises, My gifts, even My proclaimed purposes in and through you? Can you trust Me and continue to believe My promises even unto death?" God was putting Abraham's love, faith and obedience to the most severe trial.

God Calls Abraham to a Very Sad Journey

True to Abraham's already established principles and ways of life, he obeyed God, making all the necessary preparations for the journey. Should he even tell Sarah? He knew it would break her heart to have to give up Isaac. This ordeal was Abraham's alone; God was not trying Sarah's faith.

Taking with him a few young servants, the prepared wood for the altar, and a fiery torch, he and Isaac journeyed to the place which God had named. For three sorrowful days they silently walked those hot, dusty miles. Abraham's heart

149

was heavy as storms of pain and anguish buffeted his soul. As the days went slowly by, turmoil and harassing doubts from the enemy shattered his peace of mind and battered against the wall of his faith and his will. In spite of the ever-increasing blasts from the enemy, Abraham pressed steadily on, refusing to slacken his pace. Whatever God had ordained must be; Abraham would obey his God.

Finally, as Abraham looked up and set his eyes upon the chosen mountain, God confirmed to him that this was the right place. To his servants, Abraham said, "Wait here for us." Then taking his son, he added, "We will go to yonder mountain to worship, and then WE WILL COME AGAIN TO YOU." Abraham's unwavering faith in His God dared to foretell their return from that mountain, even though he clearly realized the dreadful obedience and sacrifice that yet lay ahead of them.

Just the Two of Them

Picking up the bundle of wood for the altar of sacrifice, he laid it on the back of his sturdy son. In one hand Abraham carried a blazing torch, in the other, a sharp knife. Then, Abraham and Isaac started up the final ascent. They "WENT BOTH OF THEM TOGETHER" up that rocky virgin terrain unto Mount Moriah. Alone — just the two of them — they walked through the grass and shrubs towards that Mount of Obedience and unspeakable sorrow.

As Abraham anticipated the dreadful, bloody, heart-rending scene that lay before him, a ceaseless stream of questions poured into his heart. "How can I do this? How can the Lord require it of me? Why doesn't God Himself just take my son's life and spare me this unspeakable horror? Can human mind or will force itself to do such a deed to one that is so dearly beloved? How can I take this knife and plunge it into my Isaac? I would much rather plunge it into my own heart. At that awful moment, will I even be able to maintain control of myself and not break down? Am I losing my mind?'' Grief — unknown to any other — was the grief that now crushed Abraham's spirit.

Did the birds merrily sing their daily songs as usual? Abraham heard them not; his ears could only hear the death moan of his dying son. If the mountains were beautiful in the wonder and mystery all mountains display, Abraham saw not their beauty, for his eyes were flooded with stinging tears. Did singing streams invitingly beckon them to rest awhile and listen to their songs of life, and promise of even greater life? Abraham's spirit could only groan in answer. Were the fading flowers of fall trying to encourage his spirit with their promise of a coming spring when once again they would burst forth in richest bloom? Grief had dulled his mind too much to receive such subtle ministrations. Did the exuberance and beauty of young Isaac — lightly and joyously walking on beside him — give a buoyant lift to his spirit? No! It only made him all the more sorrowful as the slow walk to the mountain devoured the remaining distance all too quickly.

Isaac's Question Is Answered

Finally, even Isaac seemed to sense there was something wrong. Where was the sacrifice that worship demanded to be placed upon the altar? Obviously they had not brought a lamb with them for the burnt offering. Did Isaac suspect? Did he have any intuition of the horrible scene that lay before both of them? ''Father,'' he said, ''behold the fire. Behold the wood. But WHERE IS THE LAMB FOR A BURNT OFFERING?''

In a voice so choked with emotion it was scarcely audible, his father answered him with a word of faith that was astounding under the circumstances, "My son, God will provide HIMSELF a lamb for a burnt offering." What a strange word! Could Abraham have known what his words really meant? Or was he inadvertently prophesying? Had faith so triumphed in his heart that it reached into a higher level where his spirit was walking up another hill some two thousand years ahead of his time?

Preparations for Worship

"SO THEY WENT BOTH OF THEM TOGETHER . . ." up, ever upwards on the pathless incline. Up over jagged rocks and through thorny brush they blazed a trail that had never before been traversed by any man. Then, reaching the summit of Mount Moriah, Abraham and his son began that horrible prelude to the holocaust. Gathering the rocks and piling them together, they made a large altar.

Still no intervening word came from God to bring answer to Abraham's troubled ponderings. Was this, then, only a test of his faith? How Abraham had wrestled with that all the way up the mountain! Was it only God's dealing, after all? Would the God of mercy and love that He had known ask of him such a horrible thing? Or was it, then, only a hallucination? Could his God truly ask something so hateful, so repulsive to his father-nature? Had he heard rightly after all? Each stone that he piled upon that altar became another piercing, burning doubt hurled into his mind by the very devil himself.

Abraham prepared the altar for the sacrifice, and placed the wood upon it. Still no voice came from heaven; he heard no word to help him. Alone, how alone he felt — remembering the sharp word God spoke to him several days before. "Take thine only son Isaac. . . ." The shocking portent, foreshadowed by God's words, increasingly became a gruesome reality to him. At last, everything was ready; Abraham could delay that tragic moment no longer. Quite obviously, his God was not there . . . nor was He coming to help him at all. Abraham stood all alone with only his will, his faith, and his determination to obey his God no matter what it might cost him. The final, awful moment arrived.

The Sacrifice Laid
Upon the Altar

Abraham took Isaac into his arms in one final heart-crushing embrace, not letting him go, lest his will should falter. In crushing sorrow, he took the cord and bound Isaac's hands and laid him upon the altar. Shocked, hurt, and frightened, Isaac entreated, "Must this sacrifice be made? You mean that God says I am to be the lamb? Is there no other acceptable burnt offering? Can God not find an easier way to express true worship?" His pathetic pleadings twisted as a knife of fire in his father's already bleeding heart. This child of promise was obedient to his father, even as his father was obedient to his Father God. Tearfully, Isaac watched and waited as his father walked over and deliberately picked up that knife. Slowly he approached his beloved son . . . an upraised knife in his hand.

Holy Writ draws a veil over that dreadful scene. The depths of these hurts and sorrows are too immeasurable, too precious for other eyes to behold. Such things are far too sacred for the profane to penetrate, too deep for human intellect to speculate upon.

All hope of divine intervention was gone. All that remained was the stubborn faith of Abraham who believed that, in spite of death, his God was able to raise up Isaac from the grave — even when such a thing had never happened before. Steadfastly and decisively Abraham walked toward his only and beloved son, believing in his God.

God Speaks Words of Release

Suddenly, *that voice* — so looked for and longed for — shattered the stillness and pierced through all the gloom. Annihilating sorrow and dreadful fear like a lightning bolt, that voice lit up the dark "stormscape," scattering forever the hounds of hell that had surrounded the mountain top.

"Abraham!" the voice said, "lay not thine hand upon the lad, neither do anything unto him . . ." (Genesis 22:12). God rewarded Abraham's faith, for as Abraham lifted up his eyes, he beheld a ram caught in a thicket by his horns. He offered it up before the Lord as a sacrifice. God released Abraham's loved son. He rewarded his unswerving faith and his devoted obedience that had never before been so tried.

In silence both father and son waited as they basked in the wonder and glory of their deliverance, worshiping together as their God-provided lamb ascended in fiery flame and smoke unto the Lord. Suddenly, there came out from heaven yet another word:

"BECAUSE THOU HAST DONE THIS THING, AND HAST NOT WITHHELD THY SON, THINE ONLY SON, IN BLESSING I WILL BLESS THEE, AND IN MULTIPLYING I WILL MULTIPLY THY SEED — AS THE STARS, AS THE SAND — AND IN THY SEED SHALL ALL THE NATIONS OF THE WORLD BE BLESSED BECAUSE THOU HAST OBEYED MY VOICE."

We Will Come Again to You

Slowly Abraham and Isaac arose, then turned and went down the mountain to the waiting servants, even as Abraham had promised they would do. And what a different journey this one was! Joy and gladness filled their hearts; peace reigned in their once troubled minds.

Having willingly given their offering in obedience to the divine command, they had truly worshiped their God in faith and in love. Now they would return home in the triumph of their faith and in the power of those mighty and far-reaching promises that would affect the whole world forever. Back home to Sarah to tell her — after everything was all over — of the tremendous things that had taken place. Back home again! And "THEY BOTH WENT BACK HOME TOGETHER!"

God Will Provide Himself . . .

"God will provide Himself a Lamb . . ." were prophetic words of far deeper import than Abraham, in his day, could possibly have realized. God had given him a preview of another Father, another beloved Son, and a journey to another mountain to which "BOTH OF THEM WENT ON TOGETHER."

What must have been in that eternal Father's heart when, unseen by Abraham, He walked up to Mount Moriah? What were the heart-breaking thoughts that echoed through the heart of the Son as He also invisibly ascended that pathless mountain with Isaac? Did the angels know how tragically prophetic that day was for the future of all heaven and earth? Could they have had any foreboding of the tremendous secrets hidden in the heart of God?

True, this story is only a portent, a picture, an Old Testament incident in the life of one of the first patriarchs. However, in the heavenlies that day was a foreshadowing; a glimpse, a portrayal of a significant event yet to come. Watching Abraham and Isaac, did the angels see how keenly God was involved with that strange scene on planet earth? Did the heavenly beings wonder at such deep divine involvement? Did they, too, ponder about the strangeness of it all? Did they hear God's words to Abraham — seemingly so out of context with all they knew their God to be? Did they realize what tragic and glorious secrets were deeply locked up in the heart of their glorious King?

Many centuries after Abraham's trial there came a day when another Father made a similar journey with his Son. That journey began in Bethlehem where "THEY, ALSO, WENT BOTH OF THEM TOGETHER." Alone they were — that Father and that Son, alone together. They walked up to the top of that Mount Moriah called Calvary. The burden of bearing "the wood of the cross" was laid upon the Son's lacerated shoulders. In His hands the Father carried the fire and the sharp cutting knife. *Silently, the Father and the Son walked along that lonely road together.*

God Prepared an Altar

Eternal decrees had predestined, and godly prophets had foretold: the journey of *this Father* and *this Son* would not end without the knife of divine justice wrathfully tearing out the life-blood of the eternally beloved Son. (Nor did the memory of Abraham's last minute deliverance bring any joy or hope of release to this Father and this Son.) Upon the altar of sacrifice, the eternal Father offered up His beloved Son, the Lamb without spot or blemish. Jesus was the burnt offering that pleased His Father. God gave His Son for the life of the world.

Today, we call the path to Moriah, the mount of God, the "via dolorosa" — the way of pain. Could human tongue or pen describe the heart of that Father and that Son as they went "both of them together" up that path to the divinely chosen place called Golgotha, the place of the skulls? When cruel men bound the Son — not with cords, but with iron spikes which nailed Him to that altar — it was because of the invisible, unbreakable bonds of filial love that had bound Him inexorably to His Father's will.

In agony Jesus pleaded in the garden, "Father, is there no other way? Is it not possible for infinite wisdom to find another sacrifice? Is there no other way than this rending which will separate us? Must death and sin divide us?" His sweat mingled with tears that fell as great drops of blood from a broken heart. Once again Holy Writ draws a veil to hide those terrible and sacred hours from us. He only allows us to hear our Lord's triumphant surrender: "Nevertheless, not My will, but Thy will be done."

"Father, here is the knife, the knife of judged sin. Here is the fire, the fire of tormenting, sinful separation from Thee. Here is the wood all laid in perfect order in the preordained form of a cross. My Father, here also is Thy Lamb; do with Me as Thou wilt. Thy will be done, not Mine, for Thou hast ordained that there is *no other way.*"

The Father had prepared the altar; He had laid the wood in order; the cross was ready. Then, with a finality of death, He took into His own hands that sword of divine justice. He plunged it into His own heart — as well as into the heart of His beloved Son. With a cry of pain at the terrible separation which made the earth quake, Jesus cried. His words ring throughout the corridors of eternity: "ELOI ELOI LAMA SABACHTHANI?" (MY GOD, MY GOD, WHY HAST THOU FORSAKEN ME?) At Calvary, sin and death separated the Father and the Son. The deadly plunge of the knife into His beloved Son's heart caused such pain of sep-

157

aration that all heaven would tremble forever at the remembrance of it. The Father and the Son were together on the cross, for "They went both of them together."

Tarry — A Promise
Has Been Given

"Wait for us," was the word to the angelic hosts. "We will go yonder to planet earth and there worship together. We will offer a sacrifice, a burnt offering, AND WE WILL COME AGAIN TO YOU."

In the simplest of words the Scriptures again draw the veil: "And there they crucified Jesus." There the Father's knife penetrated deeply into the heart of the Son; there the saving blood was shed. The altar fires burned and consumed the sacrifice. The bloody knife of divine justice was sheathed forever so that no other burnt sacrifice need ever be offered again.

Bonds Are Broken,
the Promise Released

Behold the faith of that Father! Behold the faith of that Son! Jesus believed that His Father would raise Him up even from the grave and fulfill all His promises and all His purposes. Therefore, no knife of justice, no burnt offering, no death, no shed blood, no shattered body, no grave, no hell could stop Jesus from returning. Divine justice decreed complete satisfaction; all its requirements were met at the cross. Thus, in spite of Christ's awful death, His shed blood, and the prison of the grave (even hell itself), both Father and Son fully believed They would return together to Their subjects, who were waiting for Them at the gates of heaven.

158

Believing, they waited until the third morning. Suddenly, these words thundered out from deepest heaven and reverberated unto deepest hell:

- "ARISE THOU PRINCE OF LIFE, THOU OVER-COMING POTENTATE;

- BREAK THOU THOSE ILLEGAL BONDS OF DEATH;

- SHATTER FOREVER THOSE IRON BARS OF THE GRAVE;

- TAKE TO THYSELF THY GLORIOUS BODY;

- LIVE FOREVER TRIUMPHANTLY, THOU CONQUERING LION OF JUDAH;

- TAKE TO THYSELF THY ETERNAL CROWN;

- REIGN OVER THY KINGDOMS FOR EVER AND EVER!"

At those mighty words, faith awoke triumphant. The bound Son sprang forth into eternal life, all His bonds shattered. Free forever! Triumphant love joined together again the Father and the Son. Then both of them returned up the starry, shining glory-road back home — both of them together.

Out of the depths of eternity the seven thunders sounded forth the everlasting covenant, sworn by high Godhead ruling upon the throne:

"BECAUSE THOU HAST DONE THIS THING, AND HAST NOT WITHHELD THY SON, THINE ONLY SON: THAT IN BLESSING I WILL BLESS

THEE, AND IN MULTIPLYING I WILL MULTIPLY THY SEED AS THE STARS OF THE HEAVEN, AND AS THE SAND WHICH IS UPON THE SEA SHORE; AND THY SEED SHALL POSSESS THE GATE OF HIS ENEMIES; AND IN THY SEED SHALL ALL THE NATIONS OF THE EARTH BE BLESSED; BECAUSE THOU HAST OBEYED MY VOICE. AND THE HOSTS OF HEAVEN SANG HALLELUJAH; SALVATION AND GLORY, AND HONOR, AND POWER UNTO THE LORD OUR GOD.''

BOOKS BY R. EDWARD MILLER

Victory in Adversity tells of outstanding incidences in the lives of God's servants, illustrating how victory was snatched from the jaws of defeat.

Thy God Reigneth tells of the beginning of the outflow of God's river of revival in Argentina and its flowing from 1949 to 1954 (available in U.S.A. only).

The Flaming Flame picks up the threads woven in **Thy God Reigneth** and is a sequel to that story (available in U.S.A. only).

Cry for Me, Argentina tells the story of revival in Argentina.

Books of Annie's Visions (Book I — **I Looked and I Saw the Lord;** Book II — **I Looked and I Saw Mysteries**) record the visions received by Annie and retold by R. Edward Miller. By revealing some of the hidden workings of God in the invisible behind the limits of sense and time, they help the believer to enlarge his concept of God and make the Heavenly City more real.

The Prince and the Three Beggars contains the following allegories:

> **The Prince and the Three Beggars** in an allegory of Christ and His bride. The most wretched and miserable of all creatures catches a glimpse of Supreme Love and an undaunted hope spurs her along seemingly impossible ways until she reaches Him.

> **The Little Tree** is a Biblical picture-story of what happened to Aaron's rod when it remained all night in the Holiest-of-All, and illustrates the fruit that God produces in and through the believer who is willing to wait before Him in the Holy Place.

> **The Mariposa Butterfly** portrays the small concept many people have of God and pictures in a unique way the largeness of God and the smallness of man.

For additional copies write to:

Peniel Publications
P.O. Box 68
Fairburn, GA 30213-0068
770/969-5952   U.S.A.

Make all checks payable to
PENIEL PUBLICATIONS.
No cash please.